THE ART OF
HOW TO TALK TO ANYONE

Gain Social **Confidence**, Boost **Communication** Skills, and Deepen **Relationships** & Social **Connections**

EVEN IF YOU'RE SHY

CHRIS BOUGATSIS

© **Copyright Chris Bougatsis 2024 - All rights reserved.**

The content within this book may not be reproduced, duplicated or transmitted without direct written permission from the author or the publisher.

Under no circumstances will any blame or legal responsibility be held against the publisher, or author, for any damages, reparation, or monetary loss due to the information contained within this book. Either directly or indirectly. You are responsible for your own choices, actions, and results.

Legal Notice:

This book is copyright protected. This book is only for personal use. You cannot amend, distribute, sell, use, quote or paraphrase any part, of the content within this book, without the consent of the author or publisher.

Disclaimer Notice:

Please note the information contained within this document is for educational and entertainment purposes only. All effort has been expended to present accurate, up-to-date, and reliable, complete information. No warranties of any kind are declared or implied. Readers acknowledge that the author is not engaging in the rendering of legal, financial, medical or professional advice. The content within this book has been derived from various sources. Please consult a licensed professional before attempting any techniques outlined in this book.

By reading this document, the reader agrees that under no circumstances is the author responsible for any losses, direct or indirect, which are incurred as a result of the use of the information contained within this document, including, but not limited to, — errors, omissions, or inaccuracies.

Trademark Acknowledgements:

All product names, logos, and brands are property of their respective owners. All company, product, and service names used in this book are for identification purposes only. Use of these names, logos, and brands does not imply endorsement.

ISBN eBook: 978-1-965021-00-2
ISBN Paperback: 978-1-965021-01-9
ISBN Hardcover: 978-1-965021-02-6

www.platinumwavepublishing.com

To my wonderful family and friends, who have been my unwavering pillars of strength and inspiration. A special mention to my good friend Aleks, whose support has been invaluable throughout this journey.

Contents

Introduction	1
1. Understanding the Basics of Communication	5
2. Building Your Social Confidence	25
3. Mastering Small Talk–The Art of Starting Conversations	37
4. Mastering Non-Verbal Communication	49
5. Deepening Conversations Beyond Small Talk	59
6. Overcoming Common Communication Challenges	75
7. Cultivating Digital Communication Skills	87
8. Building and Maintaining Personal and Professional Relationships	101
9. Specialized Communication Strategies for Unique Situations	111
Conclusion	121
References	127

Introduction

People are not born with a certain amount of social skills. They learn how to be social.

—Lafbe

Have you ever found yourself frozen at a social event, words clinging to the back of your throat, unable to find their way out? Perhaps you've replayed a conversation in your mind, wishing you had spoken up or expressed yourself more clearly. What about when just the thought of having to interact with people is so overwhelming that you find yourself avoiding others?

A lack of social skills isn't just a case of being shy or even an introvert. It can take over your entire life. For Sammy, communication in the office was so terrifying that she almost found herself out of work. Charlie wasn't a bad-looking guy, but he had spent his entire twenties as a single man because his low self-esteem and confidence when around others rarely got him past the first date. Sophie was the black sheep of the family, not because she looked different, but because she would never back down from an argument, unable to see anyone else's point of view.

For Sammy, Charlie, and Sophie, not being able to communicate with others left them feeling completely isolated, and the spiral only got worse. They began to dread interactions, becoming increasingly anxious days before they knew they were going to have to engage with others. Stress and anxiety built up, and all began to suffer from symptoms of depression.

Maybe you, too, have felt your relationships and connections with others becoming more and more distant. What hurts even more is that the very few people you can confide in don't understand, telling you that you just need to stop being so shy.

It's not a simple case of getting out there and overcoming your fears. At the same time, you are the only person who can transform your life and create meaningful connections that you have dreamed of. It's only natural that you need support and an empathetic guide to help you master social skills.

Personally, I have been where you are. I was a shy kid, and adults all around me said that I would "grow out of it," but that never happened. Instead, the challenges of my shyness developed into social anxiety that impacted every area of my life.

To an extent, my shyness and social anxiety have been advantageous. I was forced to research social and communication skills and experiment with the widest range of techniques possible. It's thanks to the combination of research and personal experience that I have the fortune of sharing methods such as the FORD, TED, SOFTEN, ARE, and SHARE models that have changed my relationships and my life. Each method is interwoven throughout the chapters, providing a comprehensive toolkit for effective communication, with real-life examples and scenarios that illustrate key points and make the advice tangible and actionable.

You aren't only going to discover how to talk to people. The art of communication extends far beyond this. You will soon be able to read a person or a room to make sure your words and actions match the environment. You will have the ability to know when someone is hiding their true emotions and how you can make them feel comfortable. You will find the confidence to strike up purposeful small talk and how to take that a step further to make long-lasting connections with individuals from all walks of life. You will embark on networking strategies to drive your career forward. We will even uncover digital communication tips for today's modern world to ensure you are communicating with complete confidence.

This book is your roadmap to transforming your communication skills. It holds a plethora of information crafted to equip you with the necessary tools to converse confidently in casual and professional environments. Whether you're battling shyness, seeking to polish your social prowess, or simply looking to deepen your connections, this guide is tailored to meet your needs.

Consider this: One study alone showed that 93 percent of employers consider communication skills to be more important than a potential employee's university major (Hunkins, 2022). Those with effective communication skills are more likely to achieve career success, maintain healthier relationships, and report higher levels of personal satisfaction. You, too, can achieve this!

Let's clear up a common misconception right from the start: Communication skills aren't solely innate. Nor are introverts destined to be poor communicators. This book will show you that effective communication is a skill that can be developed regardless of personality type.

So, I invite you to turn the page and step into a journey of growth and mastery in the art of conversation. Remember, every chapter you read is a step closer to becoming the confident, articulate person you aspire to be. The key to overcoming any problem is to break it down into smaller, more manageable steps. So, before expecting the unrealistic of ourselves, we will begin by looking at what communication is and why it feels impossible for some.

Chapter 1
Understanding the Basics of Communication

The single biggest problem in communication is the illusion that it has taken place.
—George Bernard Shaw

Communication is the bridge that connects us to the world around us, allowing us to express our thoughts, feelings, and ideas. However, despite its fundamental role in our lives, effective communication is often a hurdle many struggle to overcome. Whether it's the trepidation of speaking up in a meeting, the nervousness of making small talk at a social event, or simply the desire to form deeper connections with others, mastering communication is a skill that profoundly impacts your personal and professional life.

This chapter is designed to be your first step toward becoming a more confident and effective communicator. We'll explore the psychological aspects of communication barriers like social anxiety and offer practical strategies to improve your interaction skills. By understanding these basics, you'll be better prepared to navigate the complexities of both verbal and non-verbal communication in any setting.

Breaking Down the Communication Process: More than Just Talking

When we think about communicating, most of us picture a simple exchange where one person speaks and another listens. If only it were that simple! More often than not, you say something and assume the other person has taken your message on board!

True communication is far more dynamic and complex. In the real world, communication should be more like a game of tennis. Someone serves the ball to the other player; the player hits the ball back. If the first player fails to serve well, the other player is unable to hit the ball back. Only when both players are able to return a well-hit ball, or in our context, conversation, can both parties enjoy the outcomes thanks to a sender and a receiver.

For instance, imagine you're discussing a new project with a colleague. As you outline your ideas (sender), you're also observing your colleague's reactions and feedback (receiver), adjusting your message in response to their cues. This exchange ensures that communication is not just about transmitting information but about creating shared understanding and meaning. This model teaches us that communication is an active, ongoing process. It highlights the importance of feedback in shaping conversations and ensuring that messages are not just delivered but also understood as intended. How many times have you said something and the receiver has responded with a completely irrelevant response? Let's be honest: How many times have you done the same? Imagine that rare occasion when you walk away from a presentation or even a conversation with a family member, and you are proud of how you got your message across. When the other person returns the next day with the complete opposite of what you explained, you may have thought you served the ball well, but from the other person's point of view, it was way off-court.

Communication dynamics reminds me of a friend who went to live in a foreign country. She didn't speak the language but tried her best to make new friends. One new neighbor was gibbering on, and my friend just kept replying with "Yes." Ten minutes later, her new neighbor was knocking on the door, ready to go on the walk she had unknowingly agreed to. Obviously, this is a breakdown in communication due to language barriers, but the process is the same. The neighbor delivered her message perfectly, but the receiver wasn't able to interpret it successfully. Regardless of the language, the result is the same—miscommunication!

Delving deeper into the roles of sender and receiver, it's crucial to recognize that effective communication relies on this dynamic. As the sender, your role is to convey your message clearly and concisely, but this is just half of the equation. As the receiver, your role is equally important— interpreting the message accurately and providing feedback.

Barriers to Communication

In any communication process, barriers can distort or disrupt messages. These barriers can be physical, such as noise in the environment; psychological, such as preconceived notions; or semantic, like jargon or overly complex language (Leverage Edu, 2023). Each type of barrier requires specific strategies to overcome. For example, in a noisy room (physical barrier), you might need to speak louder or find a quieter place to converse. If dealing with psychological barriers, such as biases or emotional disturbances, it may help to clear the air with a candid pre-discussion to address any underlying issues. For semantic barriers, simplifying your language and avoiding technical jargon can enhance understanding.

These barriers are easy to overcome compared with emotional and cognitive barriers. On the one hand, you or the other person may enter a conversation with emotions that affect how you interpret information. Going into a conversation feeling stressed and anxious makes it harder to focus on what the other person is telling you. If you start to feel angry at what someone is saying, your thoughts will be on your emotions rather than the message. One of the hardest barriers to overcome is fear, the fear of judgment, which can make you second-guess what you want to say.

On the other hand, we all have a set of cognitive biases that shape our opinions of a person and what they are saying. Our past experiences regarding cultures, age, and even the appearance of a person can create stereotypes that influence our thoughts of a person before they speak. Because it's something we all experience, the person you are talking to is also tapping into their biases, forming opinions of you.

The context of communication plays a critical role in how messages are interpreted. Context includes the physical setting of the communication, the social relationships between communicators, and the cultural background of the participant (Lumen, n.d.). For instance, a casual remark made in a boardroom might be perceived differently than the same remark made in a coffee shop. Similarly, a message delivered in a cultural context where directness is valued (such as in the US) might be perceived very differently in a culture where indirectness is the norm (such as in Japan).

Understanding the importance of context can prevent many communication mishaps. It involves being aware of the surroundings, the relationship dynamics, and the cultural backgrounds of those involved in the communication. This awareness helps in tailoring messages in a way that they are not only heard but also respected and understood within the right framework.

With this in mind, we begin to see the layers and complexities involved in every interaction. It's not merely about talking; it's about engaging, exchanging, and evolving with every message we send and receive. Whether you're chatting with a friend or leading a meeting, remembering these elements can transform your communication from mundane to meaningful.

Overcoming Barriers to Communication: Common Missteps and How to Avoid Them

In our daily interactions, whether with friends, colleagues, or strangers, we often encounter invisible walls that can distort or block the flow of communication. These barriers, if left unchecked, can lead to misunderstandings, frustrations, and missed opportunities. Understanding these obstacles is the first step toward overcoming them and enhancing our ability to connect with others effectively.

Overcoming psychological barriers begins with awareness and then, gradually, with targeted action. If fear and anxiety are the walls you face, techniques such as mindfulness and grounding exercises can be incredibly effective. These methods help you stay present in the moment, reducing worry about possible future outcomes or past interactions. For prejudices that can cloud judgment and hinder open communication, exposure and education about other cultures or differing viewpoints can broaden understanding and reduce biases. Engaging in forums or community groups that foster diverse interactions is a practical approach to expanding your social and cultural horizons.

Step 1: Building Self-Esteem for Effective Communication

Self-esteem plays a pivotal role in how we communicate. When you feel confident, your words tend to flow more freely and assertively. Building self-esteem can start with setting small, achievable goals in your interactions. For example, if speaking up in group settings is a challenge, you might set a goal to make at least one comment in each meeting you attend. There will be more on setting goals for communication later in the chapter. Each small success builds your confidence and establishes a positive reinforcement loop. Additionally, affirmations and positive self-talk can fortify your belief in your own communicative abilities. Reminding yourself of your past successes in communication can be a powerful booster to your self-esteem. It's all too common that you are spending the majority of your energy on perceived weaknesses, and this makes it easy to overlook the communication skills you are good at.

Step 2: Coping Mechanisms for Fear of Rejection

The fear of rejection is perhaps one of the most common fears affecting communication. It can silence voices and opinions that deserve to be heard. To combat this, developing resilience is key. This can be fostered by gradually exposing yourself to situations where you risk rejection in a controlled and manageable way, thus desensitizing yourself to its impact over time. Another effective strategy is reframing rejection as a natural part of learning and growth rather than a personal failure. This shift in perspective can reduce the fear's paralyzing effect and encourage more open and authentic sharing of ideas and feelings.

Step 3: Creating a Supportive Communication Environment

Finally, the environment in which communication occurs can significantly influence its effectiveness. An environment that values openness, respect, and inclusivity can encourage more honest and effective exchanges. Creating such an environment can start with you by being mindful of how you respond to others. Showing genuine interest in others' ideas, offering constructive feedback, and acknowledging good points made by others can contribute to a more supportive communication climate. Additionally, being aware of and adjusting your communication to be inclusive of all participants, regardless of their cultural or social backgrounds, can make everyone feel valued and respected.

By addressing these barriers and working on the suggested strategies, you can enhance not only your own communication skills but also contribute positively to the interactions you engage in daily.

The Role of Listening in Effective Communication

Imagine you're in a conversation where you share something important, and the response you get is a nod or a simple "uh-huh" without any sign that the person really grasped what you said. They may have heard you, but they certainly weren't listening. The distinction between listening and hearing is crucial.

Hearing is the physiological process of perceiving sound; it's passive and does not involve thoughtful processing of the content. Listening, however, is an active, deliberate choice to not just hear the words but to understand the message and emotions behind them. While hearing is an involuntary act, listening requires directed efforts and focus. We have all had moments when someone is talking to us, and our minds are racing with what's left to be done or what to cook for dinner!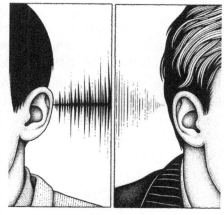

Active listening involves giving your full attention to the speaker, understanding their message, responding thoughtfully, and remembering the discussion. It's about engaging with the speaker and showing them that what they say truly matters to you.

Paraphrasing what the speaker has said and reflecting it back to them is a powerful way to show that you are not only listening but also processing the information. This can be as simple as, "So, what you're saying is..." Such a technique not only clarifies that you have understood but also gives the speaker a chance to correct any misunderstanding right there and then. Another technique is using non-verbal cues like nodding, maintaining eye contact, and leaning slightly toward the speaker, all of which signal that you are fully engaged. Asking open-ended questions that encourage the speaker to expand on their thoughts is yet another active listening strategy that can deepen the conversation.

Taking active listening to the next level, we have empathetic listening. Empathetic listening goes beyond just understanding the words or the surface message; it involves connecting with the speaker's emotions and seeing the world from their perspective. This type of listening can significantly deepen relationships and foster a greater understanding between individuals.

Imagine how differently some of your interactions could have gone if the other person had recognized your fears and anxiety and responded in a way that put you at ease.

Practicing empathetic listening involves paying close attention to the speaker's body language and tone, which often convey more than words can say. For example, if a friend is talking about a stressful situation at work but laughing it off, noticing the stress in their eyes or the strain in their laugh can prompt you to explore their feelings more deeply. This might lead you to respond with genuine concern, asking how they are really coping rather than just laughing along. This approach not only validates the speaker's feelings but also strengthens the emotional connection between you.

Empathetic listening can transform interactions in profound ways. It builds trust, reduces conflicts, and enhances the emotional well-being of both parties involved. It shows that you care not just about the conversation but about the person behind the words. As we continue to navigate through the complexities of human relationships, fostering the ability to listen empathetically is more than just a communication skill—it's a bridge to deeper, more meaningful connections.

Non-Verbal Communication: Speaking Without Words

Non-verbal communication is a fascinating yet often overlooked aspect of communication where a wealth of information is conveyed through gestures, facial expressions, posture, and even the distance we maintain from one another. Our body language often speaks louder than our words, revealing our true feelings and intentions. Recognizing and understanding these silent signals can greatly enhance your ability to communicate effectively and authentically.

Breaking down non-verbal communication, we find it consists of several key elements, each playing a unique role in how we understand and interact with each other. Body language, for instance, includes the way we hold our bodies and the micro-movements we make – a crossed arm might suggest defensiveness, while leaning in can show interest and engagement.

Facial expressions are perhaps the most immediate indicators of our emotional state. A smile can indicate openness and warmth, while a furrowed brow might signal confusion or concern. Consider a scenario where you're meeting someone for the first time. Before any formal introduction or handshake occurs, your body posture, the openness of your stance, and your facial expression have already begun to communicate. These elements create a first impression that sets the tone for the verbal conversation that follows. Two people who meet and greet each other with a warm handshake set a tone of ease. Nothing starts a conversation off more awkwardly than when one person reaches for a hand while the other leans in for two kisses!

The power of body language in reinforcing or contradicting verbal messages is immense. Consistency between what's being said and the body language accompanying it tends to enhance trust and clarity. Meanwhile, a mismatch, such as saying "I'm fine" while your body is tense and your arms are crossed, can create confusion and mistrust. Learning to read these cues accurately enables you to better understand others' intentions and feelings, even when their words may not fully disclose them.

For example, if the person you're interacting with consistently checks their watch or looks at the door, these actions might indicate their impatience or desire to end the session, regardless of their verbal assurances of being attentive. Recognizing these cues allows you to adjust your approach, perhaps by getting straight to the point or addressing their apparent discomfort directly.

Non-verbal communication is deeply influenced by cultural backgrounds, making cultural sensitivity crucial in interpreting these silent messages accurately. Gestures that are considered positive and affirming in one culture might be offensive in another. For instance, the thumbs-up gesture is commonly used in the United States to denote approval and agreement; however, in parts of the Middle East, this same gesture can be considered rude or even obscene. Gestures, such as waving, pointing, or nodding, also carry meanings that can vary significantly across different cultures (Zucchet, 2023).

Cultural variations also extend to perceptions of personal space, eye contact, and even the way emotions are expressed. In many Asian cultures, maintaining a somewhat reserved body language is seen as a sign of respect, whereas in Latin cultures, more expressive gestures and closer physical contact are norms. Being aware of these differences is essential not only in avoiding misunderstandings but also in building respectful and effective communication across diverse cultures.

How to Improve Your Non-Verbal Communication

A good starting point is to observe how your interactions vary with different people and in different settings. Pay attention to your own body language in meetings, social settings, or even in stressful situations. Are your gestures and expressions aligning with what you intend to communicate? Do you notice how your non-verbal communication can change even when talking to the same person in different environments? This will often be most noticeable with colleagues in the office and in a social setting, such as when having drinks after work.

To ensure you understand a person's emotional response is the same as their verbal message, it helps to understand micro-expressions. These are facial expressions that last for a split second, but they are much harder to fake. Here are some tips to pick up these subtle emotional communications:

- **Happiness**: the Duchenne smile or genuine smile with upturned lips and crow's feet (wrinkles) around the eyes.

- **Sadness**: the corners of the mouth are turned down, eyebrows are pulled together, and eyes may seem watery.

- **Surprise**: wide eyes, eyebrows are raised high, and the mouth may be open. Don't forget that surprise can be positive or negative!

- **Fear**: wide eyes, eyebrows raised and possibly pulled slightly together, lips are tense.

- **Disgust**: eyes are narrow, the upper lip is raised, and the nose is wrinkled.

- **Anger**: eyes are narrow, lips are tense, eyebrows are furrowed, and nostrils are flared (Van Edwards, 2024).

Practicing mindfulness can also play a significant role in managing and improving your non-verbal communication. Being fully present in the moment allows you to be more attuned to the subtleties of your own and others' non-verbal cues. A great practice for me has been people-watching. If I have the chance to get outside during a break, I find somewhere where I can just sit, focus on my breathing, and watch how others interact with each other. These moments of calm have really opened my eyes to how much we communicate without words.

Additionally, seeking feedback from trusted friends or colleagues can provide insights into how your non-verbal communication is perceived and areas where you might improve. If you aren't at the stage to seek feedback just yet, don't worry. It sounds like a cliché, but practicing in the mirror or even recording yourself can provide you with insights you haven't considered before.

Engaging in role-playing exercises can be particularly beneficial, especially when you choose a wide variety of situations. These scenarios can help you practice maintaining open body language, using appropriate facial expressions, and employing gestures that enhance rather than detract from your message. Over time, these practices can help you develop a non-verbal communication style that is not only effective but feels natural and authentic.

Understanding and mastering the nuances of non-verbal communication can profoundly impact your interactions. The ability to communicate well without words is an invaluable skill that deepens connections and enriches understanding across the spectrum of human interactions.

The Impact of Tone and Voice Modulation

Understanding how your tone of voice affects communication can be as transformative as learning a new language. The way you say something often carries more weight than the words themselves, influencing the emotional climate of the conversation and shaping the listener's perception. Think about a simple phrase like "I can't believe you did that." Spoken with a soft, warm tone, it could express genuine admiration; delivered in a sharp, harsh voice, it might convey disappointment or anger. This dual power of tone to alter message reception is pivotal in all forms of communication, from intimate chats to public speaking.

The emotional impact of tone on the listener is profound. It sets the mood and can either build trust and warmth or foster discomfort and disconnection. For instance, a manager's calm and composed tone during a stressful project can reassure and motivate the team, while a tense and sharp tone might heighten anxieties. Tone can also subtly convey sincerity, irony, sarcasm, and a spectrum of other sentiments, which listeners pick up as cues to interpret the underlying meanings of words. It's much like adding color to a black-and-white sketch, where tone fills in the emotional context that words alone might miss.

Voice modulation is the control and intentional alteration of pitch, volume, and pace in your speech (PiAcademy, n.d.). It plays a critical role in effective communication. Modulating your voice can help emphasize important points and express emotions appropriately, keeping the listener engaged. For example, lowering your pitch and slowing your pace can draw attention to a key point, signaling its importance, much like slowing down when you approach a crucial turn on the road to ensure you navigate it safely. Alternatively, increasing your pitch and pace might convey excitement or urgency, propelling the conversation forward with renewed energy.

One practical technique for voice modulation is the use of pauses. Strategic pauses can give listeners time to absorb information, generate suspense, or emphasize a point. Imagine telling a story where you pause right at the climax, the room goes silent, and everyone leans in. This moment of silence can be as powerful as the punchline itself. Additionally, varying your volume can also play a significant role; speaking softly can draw people in, creating a sense of intimacy, while a louder voice can energize a room and command attention.

Understanding vocal cues is essential not only in projecting emotions and intentions but also in interpreting those of others. Vocal cues can provide insights into a speaker's confidence, sincerity, and emotional state. A trembling voice may indicate nervousness, while a steady, even tone might suggest confidence. Being attuned to these subtleties can enhance your interpretative skills, allowing for more empathetic and responsive interactions.

Regular exercises can be incredibly beneficial for improving your vocal delivery. Just as musicians practice scales to enhance their control over instruments, you can use vocal exercises to gain better control over your voice. Try reciting a passage from a book, gradually varying your pitch to explore your vocal range, or practice speaking at different volumes and speeds to discover what feels most natural and effective for different types of communication. Recording your voice can provide valuable feedback, helping you hear what others hear and adjust accordingly.

Incorporating these techniques into your daily communication can transform mundane exchanges into impactful messages, enhancing both your personal interactions and professional presentations. Just as an artist uses different brushes and strokes to bring a painting to life, you can use tone and voice modulation to enrich your verbal communications, making them more dynamic, persuasive, and engaging.

Tying It All Together with Emotional Intelligence

There is a lot of hype around emotional intelligence at the moment, especially in the workplace, and for good reason. Emotional intelligence, or EQ, is the ability to recognize and manage your own emotions as well as recognize and influence the emotions of others. Among the many benefits of EQ, research has shown that EQ can have a positive impact on communication, even across different demographics such as gender, age, and culture (Jorfi, et al., 2014).

Active listening, empathy, and being your authentic self are three ways to begin; however, all of this begins with self-awareness. It's your own self-awareness that will enable you to recognize your emotions and turn reactions into responses through calming intense emotions.

Labeling emotions has been proven to impact the duration and intensity of them. Studies have shown that simply putting emotions into words such as "I feel anxious" can reduce the duration and intensity. At the same time, labeling more positive emotions can increase the duration and intensity (Torre & Liberman, 2018). Rather than resorting to "I'm fine," expand your emotional vocabulary and be more specific about how you feel.

Over the next few days and weeks, pay close attention to what triggers strong emotional reactions. Understanding your triggers helps you prepare in advance and avoid unnecessary events. For those you can't avoid, appreciate that between every trigger, there is a moment for you to take advantage of before you respond. It's often just a split second, but it's still enough to choose to take a few deep breaths, calm your nervous system, and respond more appropriately.

Setting Realistic Communication Goals for Self-Improvement

When it comes to enhancing your communication skills, setting goals isn't just about declaring what you hope to achieve. Your goals will provide you with clear steps to achieve what you want to and provide you with some excellent motivation along the way. Learning about effective communication is only the first step; putting the theory into practice is going to take time. If things don't always go your way, your goals will help you stay on track, focusing on the progress and not just the end result.

There are many well-known strategies for setting goals. You have probably heard of SMART goals (Specific, Measurable, Achievable, Relevant, and Time-Bound) and possibly even the GWOP method (Goal, Why, Obstacles, and Plan). Both of these strategies have helped me in the past, but I found that I needed one that covers the key concepts of effective communication. This is how I developed the SYNC GOALS system.

S - Specific

When setting communication goals, it's essential to be specific about what you want to achieve. Instead of a vague goal like "improve communication," consider specific objectives such as "communicate project updates clearly in team meetings" or "express personal boundaries assertively."

Y - Yielding

Yielding in communication means being open to feedback and willing to adapt. It involves acknowledging when communication could be improved and being receptive to suggestions from others. By embracing feedback, you can continuously tweak your communication skills and build stronger connections with those around you.

N - Nuances

Effective communication requires an understanding of nuances in language, tone, and body language. Pay attention to subtle cues such as facial expressions, gestures, and vocal inflections, as they can convey additional meaning beyond words alone. Being attuned to these nuances enables you to respond appropriately and empathetically in conversations.

C - Clarity

Clarity is key to successful communication. Aim to express your thoughts and ideas in a clear and concise manner, avoiding ambiguity or confusion. Use simple language, organize your thoughts logically, and provide relevant context to ensure that your message is easily understood by others. For more important communications, it's a good idea to prepare and practice what you want to say beforehand.

G - Genuine

Authenticity fosters trust and connection in communication. Be genuine in your interactions by expressing your thoughts, feelings, and intentions honestly and transparently. Avoid pretending to be someone you're not or concealing your true emotions, as this can undermine trust and hinder effective communication. Your confidence will grow, so this isn't the time to fake it until you make it!

O - Openness

Openness involves creating an environment where communication flows freely. Encourage dialogue, invite questions and feedback, and demonstrate a willingness to listen to differing viewpoints. By fostering an atmosphere of openness, you promote collaboration, creativity, and mutual understanding within relationships.

A - Active Listening

Active listening is a fundamental aspect of effective communication. It involves fully engaging with the speaker, demonstrating empathy, and seeking to understand their perspective without judgment. Remember, active listening includes maintaining eye contact, nodding in acknowledgment, and paraphrasing the speaker's message to ensure clarity and comprehension.

L - Learning

Communication is a skill that can be continuously developed and refined once you adopt a growth mindset. A growth mindset is when you believe your skills and abilities can be improved. Actively seek out opportunities to learn and improve your communication skills, and don't forget that setbacks aren't a sign of failure; they are moments you can learn from.

S - Support

Supportive communication involves offering encouragement, empathy, and assistance to others in their communication efforts. Be attentive to the needs of your colleagues, provide constructive feedback, and offer help when needed. A supportive environment contributes to a culture of collaboration, trust, and mutual respect, qualities that are essential in all our interactions.

Let's take a practical look at SYNC GOALS in action:

- **Specific**: I want to master public speaking skills in time for a conference in 6 months.

- **Yielding**: I need to assess my current skills and decide where I need to improve (not ignoring the skills I already have).

- **Nuances**: When talking to a larger group, my facial expressions might not be clear to everyone, but I will need to work harder on my gestures and tone of voice.

- **Clarity**: I should research my audience and make sure the vocabulary and context are relevant to the audience and used in a way that everyone will understand.

- **Genuine**: My presentation needs to include facts and figures. I need to recognize my own emotions regarding the information I am showing and not shy away from expressing my thoughts.

- **Openness**: Will I have time during my public speaking for others to ask questions, or should I plan a Q&A session for the end?

- **Active Listening**: Again, as the audience is larger, so eye contact may not be as effective. In this case, I need to improve my paraphrasing skills.

- **Learning**: I am going to break down the skills needed for public speaking. First, I want to master my presentation alone, and I will record myself after some practice. Then, I will practice with one person I trust until my confidence improves. Finally, I will practice in front of a smaller group. Each time, I will ask for feedback so that I can improve more.

- **Support**: I will prepare a handout with my contact information at the end. This will show others that I am available if they need help and give me more opportunities to practice my communication skills.

Combining the elements of SYNC GOALS allows you to create an actionable plan that can then be implemented into even smaller daily practices, as well as weekly challenges and monthly check-ins to reflect on progress and set new goals. Such a structured approach not only organizes your efforts but also makes improvement consistent.

One mistake to avoid with goals, regardless of the acronym you choose, is the importance of allowing for some flexibility. There will be things that come your way that are out of your control. Imagine if you had set your goal to meet ten new people in the early months of 2020 before the pandemic hit. With social interactions so restricted, it would have been unfair to blame yourself for not hitting this goal.

This is why breaking a larger goal into smaller steps and monitoring your progress for these smaller goals is essential. If I had left my goal of public speaking simply as it was, the chances are I would have gotten to a few weeks and had to rush the process. My plan was to master my presentation by myself within the first month. Had I not succeeded, I would have had to adjust the rest of the steps but only slightly compared to changing the entire goal. If I had succeeded, I would have been able to adjust the goals to push myself a little harder.

Now, it's your turn! First, I want you to think of three areas of communication in which you would like to improve.

1. _____

2. _____

3._____

Next, take your most important goal and plan your SYNC GOALS. Don't feel you have to do this all at once. Take a few days for consideration!

S-

Y-

N-

C-

G-

O-

A-

L-

S-

Setting goals in communication is not about rigidly sticking to a formula but about creating a framework that supports continuous growth and adaptation. As we move onto the next chapter, you will discover plenty more techniques to incorporate into your goals, especially as we uncover how to inject genuine confidence into your newly acquired communication skills!

Chapter 2
Building Your Social Confidence

Confidence is not about being superior to others; it's about being comfortable with who you are, flaws and all.
—Anonymous

Have you ever watched a confident person talking to a crowd of people, every one of them hanging on to each word they say? It's probable that you stood back at a distance, wondering if you would ever have that same skill when your heart is racing whenever someone looks as if they are going to approach you.

Excellent communication skills are all well and good, but what if you don't have the confidence to use them? Whether it's shyness or full-blown social anxiety, this chapter will give you the tools to speak with genuine confidence.

From Shy and Anxious to Sociable: A Step-by-Step Confidence Building Plan

Shyness is defined as a "tendency to feel awkward, worried, or tense during social encounters, especially with unfamiliar people" (American Psychological Association, n.d.). Some children will grow out of their shyness, but it's not guaranteed. Parenting styles, such as authoritarian and overprotective, can increase levels of shyness. Social experiences in childhood may also make it harder to grow out of.

The problems associated with shyness are often overlooked; it's almost as if people think you aren't making an effort to be more outgoing. They don't understand that the fear and panic cause you to sweat, shake, and your heart to race.

Social anxiety is an extreme form of shyness, and the fear of social situations can be paralyzing. Many symptoms are similar to extreme shyness. It's possible to start shaking and sweating, and your heart rate increases. In these cases, social interactions, whether one-on-one conversations or group situations, have triggered the body's stress response, fight or flight.

Back when cavemen were hunting, this response was essential for their survival. A rustle in the bushes ahead could have been predator or prey. In a matter of seconds, the body releases hormones that slow down digestion and redirect energy to other organs, such as the heart and lungs, so the body is able to respond. Even your sight and hearing adapt to prepare for this perceived threat. You may wonder why you need to know this; it's not like you need someone to tell you how you physically respond to social interactions! Personally, I found this information reassuring. Beforehand, I was convinced my body was working against me during these times of stress. Considering this is an evolutionary response, I realized it was just my brain working overtime to protect me.

Shyness may stem from low self-esteem and confidence, whereas social anxiety is rooted in fear of being judged, embarrassing yourself, or being criticized. Aside from the emotional strain of social anxiety, it can also cause dizziness, nausea, and, in some cases, panic attacks.

Both shyness and social anxiety can be overcome, and the better news is there is one technique that reduces fear and boosts confidence at the same time. Exposure therapy is a skill used in cognitive behavioral therapy (CBT). Exposure therapy is effective because it desensitizes the internal anxiety alarm (Raypole, 2021). Essentially, it makes the amygdala, the part of the brain that is responsible for processing threats, less sensitive.

Exposure therapy doesn't mean you just get out there. It's a gradual process that can be done with a therapist or by yourself. You may find it helpful to have a trusted friend with you if you choose to do this without a therapist, but that will depend on your level of shyness or social anxiety.

Begin by listing all your fears surrounding social situations. Now, organize this list from the smallest fear to the biggest. This is often referred to as a fear ladder (Mayo Clinic, n.d.). Here is an example:

1. Being watched when eating

2. Starting a conversation

3. Sharing my opinions

4. Large crowds

5. Meeting someone new

6. Talking in groups

Before taking the first step, it's crucial that you master your stress levels. This can be achieved through deep breathing or mindfulness. I use the grounding technique where I find five things I can see, four things I can touch, three things I can hear, two things I can smell, and one thing I can taste.

Next, take the first thing on your list and put yourself in that situation. At first, it will be terrifying, but you will notice that each time you repeat the same action, your physical and emotional responses will lessen. When you no longer react, you know it's time to move onto the next situation on your fear ladder, again repeating it until you don't respond with anxiety.

The great thing about exposure therapy is that each time you overcome a fear on your ladder, you will start to feel more confident.

Additionally, keeping a journal of your social interactions can be a valuable tool. Writing down the details of each interaction and how they made you feel helps to identify progress and areas for improvement. It's a practical way to track your growth and encourage yourself by reflecting on the strides you've made.

By understanding and addressing both the psychological and physiological aspects of social anxiety, you can begin to dismantle the barriers that it creates in your communication. This chapter lays the foundation for you to build stronger, more confident communication skills that will serve you in every area of your life.

Consider the case of Emma, a college student who struggled with severe social anxiety. Emma would avoid speaking in class or attending social gatherings, fearing she would say something embarrassing. Through CBT, Emma learned to identify and challenge her negative thoughts. She practiced scenarios with a friend before exposing herself to social situations that scared her. Gradually, her confidence grew, and over time, Emma was not only able to participate in class but also started enjoying social events she would have previously avoided.

Harnessing the Power of Positive Self-Talk

Inner dialogue can be your greatest ally or your most debilitating critic, especially when it comes to social interactions. The way you talk to yourself profoundly influences your self-esteem and confidence. Negative self-talk, such as thoughts like "I'm not interesting enough" or "I always say the wrong thing," undermines your self-worth and can cement a fearful approach to social situations. Conversely, transforming this inner narrative to a more positive and supportive tone can dramatically shift your perspective and boost your confidence.

CBT is also particularly effective in tackling the negative thought patterns that fuel social anxiety. CBT works by challenging and replacing irrational beliefs with more realistic and positive ones (Selva, 2018). For instance, if you often think, "I'm going to embarrass myself," CBT encourages you to counter this with, "Everyone makes mistakes, and that's okay." Using this technique will help improve your self-esteem as you calm your inner critic, talking to yourself with more empathy, much like a friend would.

The shift begins with awareness and is strengthened by choice. Every moment offers the opportunity to catch detrimental thoughts and reframe them into something empowering that supports your social endeavors rather than sabotaging them.

Transforming your inner dialogue requires consistent practice. It's like reprogramming a habit. Begin by observing your thoughts. What narratives do you often tell yourself about your social skills and interactions? Write these thoughts down and objectively look at how they influence your behavior and feelings. This awareness is the first step in changing the narrative.

Next, actively challenge these negative thoughts. If you find yourself thinking, "I'm too awkward," question that belief. Ask yourself, "Is this really true? Are there times I've been social, and it went well?" This questioning can help you realize that these beliefs are often based on selective or exaggerated perceptions rather than absolute truths.

Now, start to replace these negative thoughts with a more realistic phrase that is believable and grounded in reality. For example, instead of saying, "I'm great at socializing," which your brain might not believe if you're just beginning to build confidence, try, "Every time I interact, I'm improving my social skills." These positive statements should be specific and in the present tense, focusing on growth and capability.

You can also try using positive affirmations to reframe your negative thoughts. There is a ton of evidence to support the use of positive affirmations to help with negative thoughts and feelings, but it's important to understand that they may not work for everyone. One study showed that people with low self-esteem didn't benefit from positive affirmations (Weber, 2014). If you want to try positive affirmations, here are some examples:

- I am relaxed in social situations.
- I like meeting new people.
- I am comfortable around people.
- I am confident talking to others.
- I enjoy hanging out with people.
- I am calm around people.
- I like talking to people.
- I am strong and brave.

If you don't find positive affirmations to be effective, an alternative is to turn your negative thoughts into questions. Consider the difference between these two phrases:

- I am going to mess up at the meeting.
- Am I going to mess up at the meeting?

The first is an absolute declarative self-statement. You are telling yourself it's going to happen. However, in the second, the question opens more possibilities.

To integrate positive self-talk into your daily routine, establish a personal affirmation practice. This could involve setting aside a few minutes each morning to repeat your affirmations or questions, write them down, or even meditate on them. Consistency is key—make this practice as habitual as brushing your teeth. You might also consider placing post-it notes with affirmations around your living space or setting reminders on your phone to repeat your mantras throughout the day.

Finally, mindfulness, the practice of being present and fully engaged in the current moment, can be a transformative tool in regulating and reshaping your self-talk. It teaches you to observe your thoughts without attachment, recognizing them as mere thoughts that don't have to dictate your emotions or actions. Through mindfulness, you can learn to catch negative self-talk as it arises, objectively assess its validity, and choose not to engage with it, reducing its impact.

Practices like mindful breathing, our grounding technique, or meditation can enhance your ability to remain centered and calm, even in socially stressful situations. By focusing on your breath or an affirmation during meditation, you train your mind to return to a state of calm, developing a skill that you can call upon when negative thoughts try to overwhelm you during social interactions.

Visualization Techniques for Social Success

The human mind is a powerful tool, not only in the way it processes the present but also in how it can shape future experiences through visualization. Scientific studies have shown that the practice of mentally simulating outcomes can significantly enhance actual performance in various fields, from athletics to public speaking. It has also been shown to help emotional regulation, reduce anxiety, and boost confidence (Roychowdhury, 2024). Visualization, or mental rehearsal, activates the same neural networks that are involved in the actual performance of the activity, preparing the brain and body to act in accordance with the envisioned scenarios. Creating a successful visualization practice involves more than simply daydreaming about positive outcomes. It requires a structured approach where you vividly detail the scenarios in which you wish to succeed. To begin, find a quiet place where you can relax without interruptions. Close your eyes and take deep, slow breaths to center your mind and body. Once you feel calm, start envisioning a particular social situation that you find challenging. Picture the setting in as much detail as possible—the sounds, the lighting, the faces of people around you. See yourself in this setting, interacting with others confidently and calmly. Pay attention to what you are saying and how you are saying it, and observe the positive reactions of those around you. The key is to make these visualizations as realistic and detailed as possible, engaging all your senses to deepen the experience.

As you regularly practice this exercise, your brain begins to build a familiarity with these positive social interactions, just as it would through physical practice. Over time, this mental rehearsal primes you to act more confidently because your brain has 'experienced' your successful interactions repeatedly. Each session adds a layer of confidence, gradually diminishing the anxiety and discomfort associated with real-life social settings.

Visualizing success in social scenarios is particularly helpful because it allows you to tackle various interactions in a controlled mental environment before facing them. For instance, if attending networking events feels daunting, visualize yourself entering the room with a calm demeanor, initiating conversations with strangers, and leaving a positive impression. See yourself exchanging contact information and laughing genuinely with new acquaintances. By repeatedly visualizing these successful interactions, you not only enhance your social skills but also build an internal expectation of success, which can be incredibly motivating. Furthermore, mental rehearsal of challenging social situations helps you navigate and troubleshoot potential issues before they occur.

Small Wins: Celebrating Progress to Build Confidence

Imagine you're learning to play a new instrument. Every note you master, every song you play a little better than the last time, contributes significantly to your growth as a musician. Similarly, each small step you take in improving your social skills is going to make a significant difference in your social confidence. It's crucial to recognize these small achievements, as they are the building blocks of your confidence. When you acknowledge your progress, no matter how minor it may seem, you reinforce your self-belief and fuel your motivation to continue improving.

Building on the importance of recognizing your achievements, creating a personal reward system can significantly enhance your journey toward social confidence. This system acts as both a motivator and a celebrator of your progress. Start by setting clear, achievable goals for your social interactions. Maybe you decide to initiate conversations with three people at an upcoming conference, or perhaps you aim to join a group discussion in your community once a week. Each time you meet one of these goals, reward yourself with something that brings you joy and encourages you to continue. This could be as simple as a favorite coffee, an extra episode of a show you love, or time in a peaceful setting like a park or a library.

The key is to choose rewards that are meaningful and enjoyable to you but also conducive to your overall well-being. Over time, the anxiety associated with social interactions can start to diminish, replaced by the anticipation of the rewards you will give yourself. This shift can significantly alter your approach to social situations, making them less about stress and more about personal gains—not just in terms of social success but also in self-care and personal happiness.

The Role of Body Language in Exuding Confidence

Let's explore a fascinating aspect of non-verbal communication, power poses, and how adopting them can transform your self-perception and outward behavior. Psychological research, such as the influential work by social psychologist Dr. Amy Cuddy, suggests that our body language not only influences how others see us but also how we see ourselves. Aside from being a social psychologist, Cuddy is a bestselling author and keynote speaker due to her award-winning research on prejudice and nonverbal behavior. Power poses, which are open and expansive postures, can lead to increased feelings of confidence and may impact our chances for success.

In Cuddy's research report, the study outlines how high-power poses (making yourself look bigger) caused an increase in testosterone and a decrease in cortisol compared with low-power poses (Carney et al., 2010). From here, the power pose was born. After one minute, participants in the study felt less stressed, more powerful, and more likely to take risks. To perform the power pose, spread your feet so they are slightly wider than your hips and place your hands on your hips with your shoulders slightly back and your head held high.

Your posture, gestures, and movements are a mirror reflecting your emotions and thoughts to the world. Aligning your body language with a mindset of confidence involves conscious adjustments to communicate strength and openness. For instance, maintaining an upright posture not only projects confidence in others but also helps you feel more alert and poised. Similarly, purposeful gestures, like using your hands when speaking to emphasize points, can make your words more impactful and convey your enthusiasm and certainty.

Start by becoming aware of your habitual body language. Do you tend to make yourself smaller in social settings, perhaps by hunching your shoulders or avoiding eye contact? Begin to shift these habits by practicing assertive and open body language. When sitting, for example, instead of crossing your legs and arms, which can appear defensive, try to adopt a more relaxed pose with your arms on the armrests and one ankle on the opposite knee. This not only makes you appear more approachable but also affects your own perception of self-assurance. This aligns with Cuddy's research and making yourself appear bigger.

Understanding subtle cues like a quick glance away, fidgeting, or closed-off postures can give you insights into how comfortable and engaged others are with the conversation. This awareness allows you to adjust your approach—for example, by shifting the topic when you notice signs of discomfort or by stepping closer and speaking more softly when you see someone is genuinely interested but perhaps a bit shy.

Practice confident body language in environments where you feel safe and relaxed. Organize sessions where you role-play various social scenarios with a friend, practicing how to enter conversations, how to stand and use gestures effectively, and how to maintain good eye contact. Each session is an opportunity to refine your body language, making it increasingly natural for you to adopt a confident stance in real-world situations. As these behaviors become more ingrained, they'll begin to flow more effortlessly in social settings, significantly boosting your confidence.

As we close this chapter, remember that each step you take in mastering your body language is a step toward not just better communication but also a deeper self-confidence that enhances every interaction. Looking ahead, the next chapter will build on these foundations, exploring how to deepen conversations beyond small talk, helping you to forge connections that are both meaningful and fulfilling.

Chapter 3
Mastering Small Talk-The Art of Starting Conversations

Conversation about the weather is the last refuge of the unimaginative.
—Oscar Wilde

Initiating a conversation is daunting! Whether it's a room full of strangers or a new colleague at a work event, the first words can sometimes feel like the highest hurdle. But what if you could leap over this hurdle with ease? This chapter is dedicated to transforming you into a maestro of starting conversations, turning potential awkward silences into opportunities for engaging, lively interactions.

Crafting the Perfect Conversation Openers

The art of opening a conversation is akin to starting a car. It doesn't matter how sleek or powerful the engine is; if the ignition is faulty, it won't go anywhere. Similarly, the initial words you choose can set the tone for the entire interaction. An effective opener is engaging and relevant and opens the door to further dialogue. For instance, generic openers like "Nice weather, isn't it?" might work in passing but often don't lead to more substantive exchanges. Instead, try openers that invite a deeper response, such as, "I noticed you're reading [book title]. What do you think of it so far?" This not only shows that you're observant but also that you're interested in their opinion, making the conversation more engaging from the start.

Another approach is to utilize your shared context to find something relatable to comment on. If you're at a conference, for example, an opener like, "What did you think of the last speaker?" can immediately tap into your shared experience and open up a channel for a deeper conversation. The key is to craft questions that are open-ended and encourage sharing, setting the stage for a flowing conversation that can build into more personal exchanges.

While mastering openers, it's also crucial to sidestep potential pitfalls that can stop a conversation in its tracks. One common mistake is making the opener overly personal or prying, which can cause the other person to feel uncomfortable. Questions like "Why are you single?" or "How much do you earn?" are too invasive for initial interactions. Another misstep is choosing controversial topics such as politics or religion, which can lead to heated debates rather than friendly dialogue. Stick to topics that are light but engaging, saving sensitive subjects for when you have more rapport with the person.

To avoid being caught off guard without a good opener, it's helpful to have a mental list of go-to questions that can be adapted to different situations. This question bank should include a mix of light, more general questions and others that are more specific but still open-ended. Examples include:

- "What's your favorite way to spend a weekend?"
- "How do you relax after work?"
- "Would you rather travel back in time or into the future?"
- "Which book could you read again?"
- "What was the last thing that made you really laugh?"
- "Who do you wish you could see live in concert?"
- "What's the most challenging thing you have ever cooked?"
- "What's the most rewarding part of your job?"
- "What's the best thing you ever bought on Amazon?"
- "Which is your favorite social media platform?"
- "If you could choose any song to play now, which would it be?"
- "Where did you grow up?"
- "Do you have a hidden talent?"
- "Are there any apps on your phone that you can't live without?"
- "What's the best movie you've seen recently?"

Having these questions ready not only prepares you for various social settings but also helps alleviate anxiety about initiating conversations, making you more likely to engage.

It's also important to remember that when asking questions, you should not assume someone's gender, pronouns, sexual identity, or sexual preference. Using inclusive language or simply asking for someone's preferred pronouns can help create a respectful and welcoming environment.

The best way to become comfortable with starting conversations is to practice in low-stakes environments where the pressure is minimal. This could be with friendly acquaintances, during casual social gatherings, or in community settings like a book club or a cooking class. These opportunities allow you to experiment with different openers, see what works best, and refine your approach based on real reactions. Each successful interaction builds your confidence, making you more adept at initiating conversations even in more critical settings, like professional networking events or formal gatherings.

By mastering the craft of opening conversations, observing carefully, and practicing regularly, you equip yourself with the tools not just to start conversations but to start them well, setting a positive tone that can lead to more meaningful and enjoyable interactions. This skill, once honed, opens a world of opportunities for richer social engagements and deeper connections. Whether you're looking to expand your social circle, make professional contacts, or just make your everyday interactions livelier and more engaging, the ability to kickstart a conversation with ease is an invaluable tool.

The FORD Method: A Foolproof Framework for Engaging Discussions

The beauty of the FORD method lies in its simplicity and versatility. It stands for Family, Occupation, Recreation, and Dreams, with each category opening a gateway to a plethora of sub-topics, allowing you to explore various aspects of a person's life without prying too deeply too quickly (Yuko, 2024). These four topics are near-universal, meaning they are safe ways to approach small talk without the risk of offending others.

Here's how you can apply it: If you're just beginning to chat with someone, you might start with a light inquiry about their family, for example, "Where do most of your family live?" This is a safe and general question that could lead to other interesting questions. If not, you can move onto occupation and so on. Applying the FORD method effectively requires a bit of finesse, especially when it comes to balancing asking questions with sharing about yourself. It's essential to avoid making the interaction feel like an interview. For instance, if you ask someone about their occupation and they mention a recent challenge at work, share a similar experience of your own or express genuine empathy. This exchange of experiences and feelings fosters a two-way conversation, making the interaction more balanced and mutually engaging. It's about creating a give-and-take that feels natural and enriching. It's reassuring that the FORD method shines across various social settings, from casual gatherings to professional networking events. At a family reunion, for instance, tapping into the family category by asking relatives about family history or childhood memories can evoke nostalgic and warm conversations. On the other hand, at a professional conference, steering the discussion toward occupation provides a platform for sharing professional experiences and expertise, paving the way for potential collaborations or learning opportunities. The key is to adapt the method to suit the context and the people involved, ensuring the conversation is relevant and engaging.

As you continue to utilize the FORD method in your conversations, remember that the goal is not just to keep the conversation going but to make it more rewarding for everyone involved. With each practice, you'll find yourself becoming more adept at navigating social interactions, turning brief exchanges into opportunities for genuine connections and shared stories. Whether you're looking to forge new friendships, strengthen existing relationships, or enhance your professional network, the FORD method provides a structured yet flexible approach that can help transform your interactions from mundane to meaningful.

Leveraging Your Environment to Start Conversations

Envision yourself walking into a community art exhibition. The walls are covered with vibrant paintings and sculptures, each piece telling its own story. This setting is a treasure trove for initiating conversations. You might start by standing next to someone who is looking at a particular piece of art and say, "The colors in this painting are incredible, aren't they? What do you think it represents?" This approach not only breaks the ice but also immediately gives you a common ground—the artwork—to build upon. Similarly, if you're at a music festival, commenting on the atmosphere or asking someone's opinion about a band that just performed can open up a dialogue that might extend into shared musical interests or experiences at other festivals. The key is to be observant and to use your environment actively to spark conversation.

Your environment is filled with clues that can guide you toward common interests or shared experiences. This requires a bit of detective work and attentiveness. For example, if you're at a culinary workshop and you see someone wearing a T-shirt with the logo of a famous chef, that's your cue. You could start a conversation by saying, "I see you're a fan of Chef Ramsey, too! Have you tried making any of his recipes?" Similarly, at a sports event, commenting on the game or asking for opinions about a player can quickly lead to a lively conversation, given the shared context and the high emotions typically involved in such settings. The key to leveraging your environment effectively across various settings is adaptability. Each setting offers unique opportunities and requires slightly different approaches. For instance, in a professional setting like a conference, your conversation starters might lean more toward networking and learning about professional roles or industry insights, whereas at a party or a social gathering, the tone can be more casual and personal. If you're at a professional networking event, a good strategy could be to approach someone who is looking at an industry award display and start a conversation about their thoughts on the latest trends affecting your industry. On the other hand, at a casual gathering, you might comment on the host's choice of music or decor to kickstart a conversation. In each case, the environment provides you with material to craft relevant and engaging openers that are appropriate for the setting and the mood.

By becoming more attentive to the details around you and learning to use them effectively, you transform every social setting you step into—a room, a garden, a street—into a landscape of opportunities for meaningful interactions. Remember, the goal is not just to start conversations but to start them in a way that they have the potential to grow into interesting, enjoyable, and perhaps even important exchanges.

The Power of Curiosity: Asking Questions that Spark Interest

Curiosity is the engine of intellectual achievement—it's the tool that has propelled humans to learn, explore, and connect more deeply with others around them. When it comes to conversations, leveraging your curiosity can transform simple exchanges into memorable encounters. Asking open-ended questions is an art form that encourages others to share their stories and experiences, enriching the dialogue and creating a fertile ground for deeper connections.

If you have had any experience with young children, you probably had those moments when everything you say just leads to another "Why?" Despite being a little annoying, it's a shame we lose this curiosity.

This is why open-ended questions are so important as conversation starters. Of all the open questions to start with, "what" is my favorite because this encourages the most curiosity. This is followed by "when" and "where." "However," "why," and "how" should be used in a way that doesn't come across as interrogative.

While open-ended questions can unlock a treasure trove of information, follow-up questions are the tools you use to dig deeper. They can clarify or expand upon the topic being discussed. Suppose someone mentions they've been learning to play the guitar. A great follow-up might be, "How did you decide to start learning guitar?" or "What's been the most challenging part of learning to play?" This not only shows that you are listening but also that you care enough to explore their interests further.

Effective follow-up questions often mirror the emotions or key points the other person has expressed, reinforcing that their thoughts are being heard and valued. This practice not only enriches the conversation but also strengthens the relational bond by demonstrating empathy and interest.

As vital as curiosity is in conversations, it's equally important to balance it with respect for the other person's privacy and boundaries. While some may enjoy delving into personal stories or sensitive topics, others might prefer to keep the conversation light. Reading these cues correctly is crucial. If someone seems hesitant or gives vague answers to certain questions, it might be a sign to steer the conversation to a more neutral topic. The goal is to make the conversation enjoyable and comfortable for both, not to pry into areas where they might not want to venture.

A good rule of thumb is to allow the other person to lead when it comes to the depth of the conversation. You can offer your own experiences and vulnerabilities first, which might make them more comfortable opening up. Remember, every exchange is a two-way street; the goal is to exchange, not to extract.

To hone your skills in curiosity-driven conversations, consider engaging in daily practices where you challenge yourself to learn something new about someone each day. This could be as simple as asking a coworker about their current projects or a friend about their recent reflections on a book they've read.

Take a moment to reflect on a recent conversation you had. Write down the questions you asked and the responses you received. Could the questions have been more open-ended? Were there opportunities for follow-up questions that could have deepened the conversation? Don't just reflect on your areas of improvement. Remember to consider what went well in this conversation and celebrate those small wins! By mastering the art of asking the right questions at the right time, you not only make your conversations more interesting and dynamic but also build deeper connections with those around you. Whether you're chatting with a new acquaintance or deepening a long-standing relationship, letting your curiosity lead the way can open up a world of fascinating insights and shared stories. So, let your curiosity flourish, and watch as your conversations transform into rich, engaging, and memorable exchanges.

How to Approach and Exit Groups Without Intruding

Before you dive into a group conversation, take a moment to observe the dynamics. Look for body language cues. Are the participants leaning in, suggesting an intense, possibly private conversation? Or are they standing in an open circle, their bodies slightly turned outward, signaling openness to new participants? These subtle signs can tell you a lot about whether it's a good time to join in.

For instance, a group engaged in laughter, with members looking around and making eye contact with outsiders, usually indicates a more casual, open discussion. On the other hand, if group members are avoiding eye contact with outsiders or have their bodies turned inward, it might suggest that the conversation is more private or not the right time to join. Reading these cues correctly not only shows your social awareness but also helps you avoid interrupting a potentially critical discussion, ensuring your entry is smooth and welcoming.

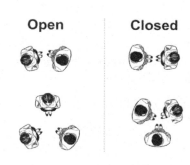

Once you've assessed that a group is open to new participants, how you introduce yourself can set the tone for your inclusion in the dialogue. Approach with a friendly smile and, if possible, catch the eye of one of the participants, giving them a non-verbal cue of your intention to join. A simple and effective way to enter is to wait for a natural pause in the conversation, then introduce yourself with a brief nod to what has been discussed, showing that you've been respectfully listening. For example, "Hi, I'm [Your Name]. I couldn't help but overhear you talking about [Topic], and I thought it was really interesting because…"

Now, as you're part of the conversation, contributing meaningfully is key to ensuring you're seen as a valuable participant. This doesn't mean dominating the discussion but rather adding insightful comments or questions that encourage deeper exploration of the topic. Show genuine interest in others' opinions and share relevant experiences that can broaden the discussion. Remember, the goal is to enhance the conversation, not redirect it. For example, if the group is discussing a recent technological advancement, sharing an article you read recently, or posing a question about potential future developments can enrich the dialogue and demonstrate your thoughtful engagement.

Knowing how to exit a conversation without awkwardness or rudeness is just as important as entering it. A graceful exit is about timing and politeness. Begin by signaling your intention to leave with a closing comment or a summary of what you appreciated about the discussion. You might say something like, "I've really enjoyed this discussion about [Topic], especially your insights on [Specific Point]. I have another engagement/meeting to get to, but I hope to continue this conversation another time!" This not only signals your departure but also leaves the conversation on a positive note, expressing appreciation for the exchange and openness to future interactions.

Imagine entering a group conversation smoothly with a well-timed comment and exiting with a compliment that leaves everyone smiling. Contrast this with barging into a discussion without acknowledging the ongoing topic and leaving abruptly without a word. The difference in reception and perception is profound. By mastering the art of entering and exiting conversations gracefully, you not only improve your social interactions but also build a reputation as a considerate and charismatic individual.

Overcoming the Fear of Rejection in Social Interactions

Have you ever felt a twinge of anxiety at the thought of walking up to someone and starting a conversation? You're not alone. Many of us have felt the cold grip of fear when the possibility of rejection looms in social settings. This fear isn't just about discomfort; it's deeply rooted in our basic human need to belong and be accepted. Understanding this fear is the first step toward overcoming it and transforming how we interact with the world around us.

The fear of rejection is often rooted in our evolutionary makeup—historically, our survival depended on our integration into groups, and social acceptance is just as critical today. The sting of rejection, whether real or anticipated, can trigger responses similar to physical pain. It's no wonder that the mere thought of rejection can prevent us from reaching out. However, it's crucial to recognize that this fear often exaggerates the consequences of a social snub. Realistically, a conversation that doesn't pan out is unlikely to have any significant long-term impact on your life. By acknowledging this, you can begin to see rejection as a momentary hiccup rather than a profound failure.

The magic happens when you start to reframe rejection not as a mark of failure but as a valuable learning tool. Each interaction gives you insights into what works and what doesn't, helping you refine your approach. Think of each conversation as an experiment; the more you engage, the better you understand the dynamics of social exchanges. Did someone not respond well to a particular topic? That's a learning point, not a failure! Maybe next time, you'll steer the conversation differently. This mindset turns the sting of rejection into a constructive force that builds your social skills over time.

When you feel the fear of rejection creeping in, grounding techniques can be incredibly helpful. These are methods that bring your focus back to the present moment, helping you manage anxiety and stress. A simple yet effective technique is focused breathing. Before approaching someone, take a few deep, slow breaths. This not only helps calm your nerves but also centers your mind, making you more poised to initiate conversation.

Set realistic expectations when you consider the conversations you wish to have. Not every conversation will lead to a deep connection or friendship, and that's perfectly fine. By setting your sights on simply having a pleasant exchange or learning something new, you reduce the pressure on yourself, making the fear of rejection less daunting.

Building resilience to rejection is like strengthening a muscle—it develops with practice and patience. Start with low-risk environments where the stakes are not too high. This could be chatting with a barista at your local cafe or striking up a conversation in a community class. These scenarios provide a safe space to practice and build up your confidence. Don't forget previously learned strategies such as gradual exposure and rewarding yourself for the small wins. Did you manage to start a conversation, even if it didn't go as planned? That's a victory in itself.

Desensitization is another effective technique. This involves gradually exposing yourself to increasingly challenging social situations, which can help normalize the experience of rejection. Begin by asking questions you know will likely have a positive response, and slowly work your way up to more challenging interactions. Over time, this practice reduces the fear associated with rejection.

Positive reinforcement plays a crucial role here as well. Celebrate your courage to engage, regardless of the outcome. Reward yourself for these small wins—perhaps with a favorite treat or activity, reinforcing the positive behavior.

As you navigate through these strategies, remember that rejection is a universal experience; it does not reflect your worth or define your capabilities. Each conversation is a step toward becoming more adept in your social interactions, equipped not just with better conversational skills but also with a resilience that enriches your social life and your understanding of human connections.

Looking ahead, the next chapter will delve into mastering the nuances of non-verbal communication, a critical component that complements and often speaks louder than words. By understanding and utilizing non-verbal cues effectively, you can enhance your communicative competence, ensuring your messages are not just heard but also felt and understood.

Chapter 4
Mastering Non-Verbal Communication

The most important thing in communication is hearing what isn't being said.

—Peter F. Drucker

Scientists have tried to put a figure on the importance of non-verbal communication. Most significantly, Albert Mehrabian found that seven percent of communication was based on words, 38 percent on vocals, and 55 percent on non-verbal signs (World of Work Project, n.d.). This has since been disputed. After all, if you consider some of the greatest speeches of all time, we don't consider how the message was delivered. We remember the words.

Nevertheless, experts still agree that non-verbal communication is crucial for effective communication. Think about the number of miscommunications we have today because of technology that misses this fundamental human element!

Though we have touched on body language, it's time to go back to your park bench or other area for people-watching as we take mastering non-verbal communication to the next level.

Understanding Personal Space

Personal space, the physical distance we maintain in interpersonal interactions, varies significantly across different cultures and individual preferences. Typically, this space is divided into four zones: intimate, personal, social, and public. Intimate space is reserved for close friends, family, or romantic partners. Personal space is for interactions with good friends and acquaintances. Social space is used in settings like workplace meetings or gatherings with strangers, and public space is for public speaking or large groups (Rakel, 2012). Here is an approximate idea of personal space distances, but please don't feel the need to get the tape measure out:

- **Intimate**: 18 inches
- **Personal**: 1.5 to 4 feet
- **Social**: 4 to 12 feet
- **Public**: 12+ feet

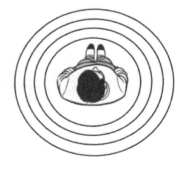

Respecting these zones is crucial for comfortable and effective communication. Invading someone's personal space can make them feel uncomfortable or threatened, leading to a communication breakdown. Conversely, standing too far away might be perceived as disinterest or detachment. Being attuned to the context and the other person's comfort with proximity can help you navigate personal space more adeptly, making your interactions smoother and more positive.

Observing and adapting to others' non-verbal cues regarding personal space is a key skill in non-verbal communication. If you notice someone backing away slightly as you step closer, it's a clear sign to increase the distance between you. Similarly, if someone seems to be leaning in, they might be comfortable with less space. These cues are often subtle, but they're critical for respecting boundaries and fostering mutual comfort in communication.

Not All Body Language Is Created Equal

One of the most telling aspects of non-verbal communication is the consistency, or lack thereof, between someone's words and their body language. When someone's words match their non-verbal cues, it tends to enhance trustworthiness and clarity. For example, if someone says they're happy while smiling and maintaining open body language, their message feels congruent and sincere. However, if someone claims to be fine but is slouching and avoiding eye contact, there might be more to the story. Recognizing these discrepancies can alert you to the complexities of a person's emotional state or intentions, providing a deeper and more nuanced understanding of their communication.

Cultural context plays a significant role in how non-verbal cues are interpreted. For instance, the meaning of eye contact varies widely across different cultures. In some Western cultures, steady eye contact is associated with confidence and honesty, while in many Asian cultures, it might be seen as confrontational or disrespectful. Similarly, gestures like the thumbs up can be positive in some countries and offensive in others. Being culturally aware not only helps you avoid miscommunications but also shows respect for diverse customs and practices, enriching your interactions with people from different backgrounds.

As well as cultural differences, it's important to remember that body language isn't going to be exactly the same for everyone. Let's take blinking as an example. The average person blinks between 15 and 20 times per minute. Excessive blinking can be a sign of lying, but it may also be caused by someone who is suffering from allergies. Some people may just naturally blink less. This is why, for closer relationships and those that you spend more time with, it's wise to get a baseline first so that you know what is considered normal for them.

On a similar note, one non-verbal cue may not be enough to complete the whole picture. This is why you should look for groups of movements, known as clusters. For example, a smile could mean that someone is happy, but it could also mean surprise or contempt. To know if a person is genuinely happy, you would look for the crow's feet around the eyes, relaxed shoulders, and leaning slightly inward.

I know this sounds like an awful lot to take in, but with time and practice, reading a wide range of people's non-verbal cues becomes second nature.

Let's take this opportunity to have some fun. Find a few video clips on YouTube that provoke different emotions. Aim for something funny, something a little disgusting, something scary, and something surprising. Ask a friend or family member to watch the different clips while you observe their reactions. You may want to record them so you can replay these reactions and really focus on the smaller details, such as their micro-expressions.

The SOFTEN Model of Approachability

Imagine walking into a room and, without saying a word, you already have people leaning toward you, interested in what you might have to say. This isn't magic—it's the power of non-verbal cues crafted into a simple mnemonic: SOFTEN (Newell-Legner, n.d.). Let's break it down:

- Smiling is universal. It's the quickest way to show friendliness and warmth.

- Open Posture, free from crossed arms or legs, signals that you are open to communication and not closed off or defensive.

- Forward lean slightly toward the person you are engaging with to show interest and engagement in the conversation.

- Touch, such as a brief hand on the shoulder or a handshake, can reinforce connection, though it's important to be mindful of personal and cultural boundaries regarding touch.

- Eye Contact shows confidence and sincerity.

- Nodding can signal agreement or encourage the speaker to continue.

Together, these elements form a powerful toolkit that can transform your interpersonal interactions across various contexts.

In personal settings, such as meeting friends or attending family gatherings, SOFTEN can make you come across as more present and connected. It's easy in our digital age to forget the impact of a warm smile or a direct look in the eyes when so much of our communication happens through screens. By consciously applying the SOFTEN model in these informal settings, you not only enrich your relationships but also enhance the quality of the interactions, making them more memorable and meaningful.

In professional environments, the stakes are often higher, and the pressure to make a good impression can be daunting. Here, the SOFTEN model serves as a subtle yet powerful tool to foster positive first impressions. Whether you're in a job interview, leading a meeting, or networking, integrating elements like a firm handshake (Touch), steady eye contact, and a genuine smile can set a tone of confidence and accessibility. These cues encourage trust and openness in communication, paving the way for more fruitful professional relationships and opportunities.

Eye Contact: Balancing Intimacy and Respect

Eye contact is a profound element of human interaction that helps to establish trust and mutual understanding. When someone meets your gaze, it often signals attentiveness and interest, making you feel acknowledged and heard. On the other hand, when someone avoids eye contact, it can sometimes be interpreted as disinterest, deceit, or even discomfort. This dual capability of eye contact, to draw people together or to push them apart, makes its correct application in conversations incredibly vital.

Maintaining the right amount of eye contact is crucial because it can greatly influence the dynamic of a conversation. Too little, and you risk appearing disengaged or insincere; too much, and you may seem overly intense or confrontational. The balance you strike can enhance communication, making interactions smoother and more meaningful.

Striking the perfect balance in eye contact is akin to a dance—knowing when to step forward and when to step back. It's about being attentive to the other person's comfort and response. If you notice someone repeatedly breaking eye contact and looking away, they might need more space, and it could be a good idea to lessen the intensity by also occasionally looking away. This can make the conversation feel more relaxed and less like an interrogation.

Improving your eye contact skills can be as simple as practicing with friends or family members. One effective exercise is the "three-second rule." During conversations, make eye contact for three seconds at a time before briefly looking away. This duration is generally enough to show engagement without making the other person feel uncomfortable.

If you find yourself in a situation where you are discussing something deeply personal or sensitive, maintaining steady, gentle eye contact can reassure the other person of your sincerity and empathy. It shows that you are fully engaged and respectful of the conversation's emotional depth. However, it's crucial to remain aware of the other person's cues. If they seem uncomfortable with sustained eye contact, it's respectful to adjust accordingly.

This is especially true for different cultures. In many Western cultures, strong eye contact is often associated with confidence and honesty and is generally considered a positive trait. However, in many Asian and some African cultures, too much eye contact, especially with someone of a higher status or the opposite gender, can be seen as disrespectful or aggressive (Raeburn, 2023). Therefore, understanding these cultural nuances is essential, especially in our globalized world, where interactions with people from diverse backgrounds are common.

When engaging with individuals from cultures different from your own, a good practice is to observe and mirror their use of eye contact. This not only shows cultural sensitivity but also helps establish a comfortable communication flow. If you're unsure, it's perfectly acceptable to ask about or research cultural norms regarding eye contact ahead of any important meetings or interactions. This preparation shows respect and mindfulness, qualities that are universally appreciated and can only enhance interpersonal relations.

The Subtle Art of Mirroring for Rapport Building

Mirroring is a powerful tool for your social toolkit, often operating just below the conscious level but with profound effects on communication and connection. Mirroring involves subtly mimicking another person's body language, gestures, speech patterns, or attitudes. This psychological phenomenon is rooted in the brain's mirror neuron system, which is thought to be crucial for empathy and understanding others' emotions. When you mirror someone during a conversation, you're essentially sending a signal that says, "I'm like you; we are in sync." This can lead to increased feelings of trust and a sense that you are both on the same wavelength, which is invaluable in both personal and professional interactions.

Imagine you are discussing an important project with a colleague who speaks in a calm, measured way and often pauses to gather thoughts. If you mirror this speaking style instead of interjecting rapidly, you likely increase mutual comfort and understanding, paving the way for a more productive and harmonious interaction. Mirroring can be as simple as adopting a similar posture or as complex as reflecting someone's mood or emotional state. When done skillfully, it fosters a connection that feels both natural and engaging, enhancing the depth and quality of different interactions.

In personal relationships, mirroring can deepen bonds and show empathy and support without overt gestures. For instance, mirroring the enthusiastic tone of a friend sharing good news can enhance their feeling of being understood and celebrated. In professional settings, mirroring can help in negotiations or team interactions by aligning your non-verbal cues with those of others, promoting a sense of agreement and cooperation. During networking events, mirroring the body language of a new acquaintance can quickly build rapport, making the conversation flow more smoothly and leaving a positive impression.

Each context demands a different aspect of mirroring. In personal settings, emotional mirroring and reflecting on feelings and attitudes can be more important. It shows that you are emotionally attuned to the other person. In professional environments, mirroring body language and speech patterns often takes precedence, as it helps establish a professional rapport and shows that you are engaged and attentive. While mirroring can be incredibly effective, there's a fine line between subtle mirroring and overt mimicking, which can come off as mocking or insincere if not handled delicately. The key to successful mirroring lies in subtlety and naturalness. It's not about copying every gesture or mimic; it's about capturing the essence of the other person's behavior. For example, if someone speaks softly, you might lower your voice slightly in response. If they lean forward when they speak, you might lean in a bit, too, showing engagement. These minor adjustments can make a big difference in how your interactions are perceived.

It's also important to keep your mirroring spontaneous and varied. If you mirror every single action or tone, it might seem like you're parroting the other person, which can feel unsettling to them. Instead, focus on mirroring the overall demeanor or key gestures that seem most central to their communication style. This approach keeps your interactions genuine and ensures that the mirroring enhances the conversation without dominating it.

Begin practicing with friends and family so that you don't risk upsetting or offending those you aren't as close to. It's crucial to practice mirroring with ethical considerations in mind. Always use mirroring to foster positive interactions and not to manipulate or deceive. The goal of mirroring should be to enhance understanding and connection, not to gain an unfair advantage or to coerce. Respect for the other person's feelings and boundaries should always be your guiding principle when employing this technique, regardless of whether it's your partner or colleague.

Using Gestures to Reinforce Your Message

Imagine you're telling a story about the most exhilarating adventure you've ever had. Now, picture telling that same story but with your hands stiffly by your sides, hardly moving an inch. Gestures add a dynamic layer to our stories, emphasize our points, and can even make our words more memorable. Whether it's a simple nod, a grand sweeping of the arms, or a subtle pointing of a finger, each gesture enriches the tapestry of our verbal expressions.

Gestures can be broadly categorized into several types: illustrators, emblems, regulators, and adaptors (Kuhnke, 2011).

- Illustrators are gestures that accompany speech and help clarify or emphasize verbal messages. For instance, you might spread your arms wide when talking about the vastness of the ocean.

- Emblems are gestures that can stand alone as words or phrases without verbal accompaniment, such as a thumbs-up signifying approval.

- Regulators control the flow of conversation; nodding can encourage a speaker to continue, while a hand-up might signal them to stop or pause.

- Adaptors are usually responses to physical or emotional needs, like twirling hair when nervous or adjusting glasses when introspective.

Each type plays a unique role in communication, and understanding when and how to use them can greatly enhance your ability to convey your message. For example, using illustrators when explaining complex information can help clarify your points, making them easier to grasp. Emblems, when used appropriately, can add a cultural or colloquial flavor to your interactions, often making them more relatable and grounded.

Incorporating gestures into your communication style should feel natural, not forced. Start by observing how others use gestures. Notice which movements seem to convey confidence and clarity and which ones distract or confuse. You can gradually start incorporating similar gestures into your own communication, especially those that feel natural to you and align with the message you're trying to convey. It's also important to consider the context and the audience; what works in a casual conversation with friends might not be suitable in a formal business presentation.

Much like eye contact, balance is key. Too few gestures can make you seem stiff and unengaging, while too many might distract from your message. Aim for a middle ground where your gestures enhance rather than overshadow your words.

Let's put gestures into practice with the "silent story" challenge. Try conveying a simple story or message using only gestures; no words are allowed. This can help you understand the power of non-verbal communication and improve your ability to use gestures more expressively. Over time, these practices will help you become more adept at using gestures naturally, enhancing both the clarity and impact of your communication.

As we wrap up this exploration of non-verbal communication, remember that each gesture, each facial expression, and each stance plays a crucial role in painting the full picture of your communicative intent. Moving forward, the next chapter will delve into overcoming common communication challenges, providing you with strategies to navigate through conversational obstacles with grace and effectiveness.

Chapter 5
Deepening Conversations Beyond Small Talk

A real conversation always contains an invitation. You are inviting another person to reveal herself or himself to you, to tell you who they are or what they want.

—David Whyte

Now, I can look back and laugh at myself, but at the time, I felt like such a fool. I had managed to overcome my anxiety and approach a person to talk to. I got the first open-ended question out, and they replied, asking me the same question, and I replied. Then, the most uncomfortable wave of silence came over us. So that this doesn't happen to you, the next stage of mastering effective communication is to discover how to turn an excellent introduction into meaningful conversations.

The Art of Transitioning From Small Talk to Deep Conversations and Being Vulnerable

The key to deepening conversation lies in recognizing those fleeting moments when surface chatter can organically shift into something more profound. These are often subtle, like a pause after a laugh or a reflective comment that hints at broader concerns or dreams. To master this, pay close attention to emotional undertones or topics that evoke more than casual interest. It could be a mention of a hobby that lights up their eyes or a thoughtful sigh when discussing work. These are signals that there's more beneath the surface, waiting to be explored. Engaging with these cues shows that you're listening sincerely and that you care about their experiences and feelings, setting a foundation for deeper interaction.

Open-ended questions are a good starting point to discover what a person is passionate about, but you can also ask questions that will help you find common ground. Imagine you are both in a cafe; the chances are pretty high that you both like coffee. The first open-ended question could be, "What's the best coffee you have ever tried?" Let's say the response is, "There is a cool Italian bar two blocks over that has the best espressos." You then have the option to lead the conversation in a number of directions: the bar, espressos, Italy, or travel. If the conversation about espressos doesn't spark much of an interest, you can redirect it with a follow-up question on travel.

For a conversation to be able to go deeper, you need to consider the environment you are in and, more importantly, whether the other person is comfortable in that environment. A party might provide a relaxed space to talk, but are you and the other person comfortable about sharing more personal information here, or would it be more appropriate to have a quiet location?

Time is also an important factor. Meaningful conversations can't be rushed. If you reach a point where you have found common ground but don't have the time for follow-up questions, let the person know that you want to find out more and make a plan to do so.

Vulnerability may feel like a weakness, but it's often the bridge to a deeper connection. It involves sharing your own experiences, worries, or dreams, revealing your authentic self. By opening up, you signal that it's safe for the other person to do the same.

To embrace vulnerability, start with sharing something personal but not overwhelming. For example, you might share a mistake you made and what you learned from it or how a certain book profoundly touched you. While you want the conversation to go deep, you don't want to overshare details of your personal life too early on and risk the other person feeling uncomfortable.

Remember that the joke you tell may not be funny, or someone may disagree with your opinion, but that is all part of sharing your vulnerability. The biggest barrier to deeper conversations is that lack of connection, and it's hard to connect with someone who comes across as perfect.

Using the TED Method to Share Stories and Experiences

Did you know that 90 percent of decision-making is based on emotions? The ability to tell a good story can provoke all kinds of emotional responses, but the brain does more than just feel the story we listen to. Neuroeconomist Paul Zak discovered that when we listen to stories, the brain releases oxytocin (Zak, 2014). Known as the love hormone, oxytocin is also the trust hormone. This signals the brain that we are okay and we are in an environment that is safe. Nevertheless, not everyone is a naturally born storyteller.

The TED method simplifies the storytelling process into three digestible parts: Tell, Explain, and Describe (Lee, 2023).

- Tell what happened, set the stage, and introduce the context or characters. This is your hook, grabbing interest with the basic premise of your story.

- Explain the actions or the core of the story, delving into what you did, how others responded, and what was at stake. This is where the meat of your narrative lies, offering insights and the sequence of events.

- Describe the outcome and your reflections, providing closure and personal insights, which add depth and meaning to the story.

For example, if you're sharing a story about overcoming a challenge at work, you start by setting the scene (Tell): "Last year, I was tasked with leading a project that was struggling to meet its deadlines." Then, move into the actions taken (Explain): "I had to find a way to motivate the team and streamline our processes. It involved several strategy meetings and late nights." Conclude with the outcome and your reflections (Describe): "The project was a success, and it taught me a lot about team dynamics and leadership under pressure."

To craft stories using the TED method that resonate and hold your listener's attention, focus on the sensory details and the emotions involved. The 'Describe' part is crucial here—it's not just about what happened but how it felt. What was the atmosphere? How did your heart race with excitement or anxiety? Describing these elements brings your story to life, making it relatable and memorable.

Let's say you're sharing an experience about a trip that changed your perspective. Describe the smells of the spices in the local market, the sounds of the city waking up, or the warmth of the sun on your skin as you climbed a mountain. These descriptions do more than paint a picture; they transport your listener to that moment with you, creating a shared experience.

To encourage reciprocal sharing, ask an open-ended question regarding the situation so that the listener can go on to share their experiences. This can once again pave the way to discovering more shared interests.

Practice the TED method in everyday conversations; start by recounting small experiences using this framework. Perhaps share about a new restaurant you tried, a movie you watched, or an interesting book you just finished. Use the TED structure to organize your thoughts and deliver a clear, engaging narrative. For a more interactive practice, organize a storytelling night with friends or family where everyone prepares a short story using the TED method. This not only makes for a fun evening but also hones your storytelling skills in a supportive environment.

Advanced Active Listening: The Key to Deeper Conversational Connection

Advanced active listening goes beyond just hearing words; it involves tuning into the emotional frequencies behind those words, interpreting subtle undertones, and responding in ways that validate and empathize with the speaker's feelings and perspectives. The first step in mastering this skill is recognizing the emotional content of conversations. This involves paying attention to more than just the semantic content. For instance, if someone talks about being overwhelmed at work with a laugh, the real clue to their emotional state isn't the words or the laugh but perhaps the slight strain behind their smile or the way their eyes avoid contact. In these moments, your ability to listen deeply can guide you to respond in ways that acknowledge the speaker's unstated stress or anxiety. You might say, "It sounds like you're juggling a lot right now. Want to talk about it?" Such responses not only show that you are listening but that you care enough to read between the lines, offering a space for deeper exploration of their feelings.

Responding empathetically is key in active listening, especially when conversations delve into more personal or emotional territories. Empathy in your responses reinforces a speaker's feelings, validating their experiences and encouraging them to open up further. To respond empathetically, focus on mirroring the emotions of the speaker with your words and non-verbal cues. If someone expresses sadness, your face, tone, and words should reflect understanding and concern. You might respond with, "That sounds really tough. I'm here if you need to talk about it," which shows solidarity and support. Another technique is to paraphrase what they've said, not just literally but emotionally. This could look like, "It seems like that situation left you feeling really sidelined," which not only shows you're listening but also that you're feeling with them.

Notice how these responses to another person's emotions validate their feelings. Avoid phrases that are considered toxic positivity, such as "It could be worse" or "Look on the bright side." We have all been guilty of toxic positivity at some point because society only encourages positive vibes. However, these phrases only encourage people to suppress their emotions and not share, the opposite of an empathetic response!

Sometimes, people aren't sharing their stories because they want advice or to be told what to do. Often, they just need to be heard and understood without the fear of judgment. This is when they need your advanced active listening skills more than ever!

The SHARE Model: Building Empathy and Understanding

When you think about the conversations that have truly made a difference in how you connect with others, there's often a deeper layer of empathy and understanding. This is where the SHARE model comes into play, providing a structured approach to enriching conversations by fostering empathy and deepening mutual understanding. SHARE stands for Seek, Humor, Ask, Reveal, Encourage, and each component is a step that contributes to building a bridge between mere acquaintance and genuine connection. Let's take a closer look at each step!

Seek

Seek involves actively seeking to understand the other person's perspective. By seeking to understand their experiences, you validate their feelings and thoughts, which is the cornerstone of empathy. For instance, if someone is discussing a difficult work situation, instead of immediately offering advice or sharing your own similar experiences, you first seek to understand by asking questions like, "What was that like for you?" or "How did that situation make you feel?" This shows that you value their perspective and are not just waiting for your turn to speak.

Humor

Humor plays a crucial role in lightening the atmosphere and making the conversation more enjoyable and less intimidating. Humor should be used sensitively and appropriately, ensuring it's inclusive and not at the expense of others. It can be a wonderful way to break down barriers and add a moment of lightness to the conversation, making it easier for people to open up. Laughing together can create a shared experience that enhances bonding. Laughing has also been shown to reduce cortisol in the bloodstream and increase levels of oxytocin (Neuroscience Leadership Institute, 2020).

Ask

The 'Ask' component encourages you to ask open-ended questions that prompt deeper reflection and sharing. These questions should be framed in a way that encourages the other person to express their thoughts more fully, providing you with further insight into their feelings or opinions. Questions like, "What motivates you to pursue this?" or "Can you tell me more about that experience?" invite elaboration and demonstrate that you are engaged and interested in understanding more deeply.

Reveal

Reveal is about sharing your own experiences or feelings in a way that mirrors the vulnerability or openness shown by the other person. This reciprocal sharing is crucial in deepening relationships because it moves the conversation beyond one-sided disclosure to a mutual exchange of personal insights. When you reveal your own experiences in response to theirs, it can validate their feelings and show that they are not alone in their experiences, which strengthens the bond of mutual understanding and trust.

Encouragement

Finally, 'Encourage' is about supporting and affirming the other person's feelings or actions. This could be through verbal affirmations, nods of understanding, or expressing appreciation for their sharing. Encouragement helps to build confidence and reinforces a positive loop in the conversation where both parties feel appreciated and valued.

The SHARE model is versatile and can be adapted to both personal and professional settings. For example, in a conversation with a friend who is going through a tough time, using humor to gently relieve tension, asking insightful questions, and sharing your own similar experiences can make them feel heard and supported.

In professional settings, SHARE can be instrumental in building rapport with colleagues and clients. For instance, encouraging a team member's efforts, seeking their input on a project, and sharing relevant experiences can foster a collaborative and empathetic work environment. This not only improves team dynamics but also enhances productivity and job satisfaction.

Practice is key to effectively integrating the SHARE model into your daily communications. Consider setting up role-play scenarios with friends or colleagues to refine your use of each component. You could simulate a scenario where one person shares a recent challenge they faced. Reflect on each step, discussing what worked, what could be improved, and how each component affected the depth and quality of the conversation.

Navigating Sensitive Topics with Tact and Respect

Jessie had just arrived home after voting when her mother-in-law turned up, and without even a "Hello," she asked who Jessie had voted for. This doesn't sound like much, but Jessie had grown up in a family who didn't discuss politics because it caused too many debates, so for her, the question was a huge invasion of privacy. What's more, she had voted for the opposite party and knew her mother-in-law would have plenty to say about this!

Sensitivity can vary widely among individuals; what might be a casual topic for one could be a minefield for another. Here are some potential topics that need to be handled with tact and respect:

- Religion
- Politics
- Health

- Gender
- Finances
- Sex
- Death
- Drugs
- Appearance

Key indicators that a topic is sensitive include hesitance in the speaker's voice, a sudden shift in body language, or even direct statements indicating discomfort. Paying attention to these signs can help you gauge when a topic might be entering sensitive territory.

Moreover, cultural, social, and personal backgrounds, like in the case of Jessie, play significant roles in what is considered sensitive. For example, gun control could be more of a sensitive topic in the US, but in the UK, Brexit can still stir up some intense emotions. While it's impossible to know all the potential sensitivities of each person you converse with, being aware of broad cultural and social contexts can provide valuable clues. For example, topics involving personal beliefs, family issues, or personal finances often require more careful handling. When in doubt, approach with openness and a readiness to shift the conversation if you sense discomfort.

Once a sensitive topic arises, navigating it with empathy and care is paramount. Begin by setting a respectful tone. This can be achieved by using non-confrontational and open-ended language, allowing the other person space to express their views without feeling cornered or judged. Phrases like "I understand this can be a complex issue; I'd love to hear your perspective" invite sharing and signal that you're approaching the conversation with respect and an open mind.

Sometimes, despite best efforts, a conversation may become too heated or uncomfortable. This is where setting boundaries becomes essential. It's okay to steer the conversation away from topics that seem to cause distress or conflict. You can gently redirect with phrases like, "I think we might see things differently on this topic. Perhaps we should switch to something less charged," or "I value our relationship and feel this topic might be putting stress on it. Let's talk about something else." It's perfectly okay to let others know that you are not happy discussing certain topics. Jessie replied to her mother-in-law with a simple "Sorry, I make it a habit not to talk about politics with friends and family."

Setting boundaries isn't just about stopping the conversation; it's about preserving the relationship and ensuring that interactions remain respectful and constructive. It demonstrates maturity and respect for the emotional well-being of both parties involved.

Mistakes happen, and you might find yourself having said something that upsets the other person. When this occurs, the ability to apologize sincerely and correct your course is invaluable. A genuine apology can mitigate damage and show your commitment to a respectful relationship. For instance, if you inadvertently make a comment that offends, a prompt apology such as, "I'm sorry, I didn't mean to upset you with my comment. I appreciate you sharing your feelings on this, and I'll be more mindful in the future," can help to ease tensions and demonstrate your respect for their feelings.

In these moments, it's crucial to listen to why the person felt hurt and to learn from the experience. This not only prevents future missteps but also deepens your understanding and respect for diverse perspectives and sensitivities.

Let's wrap this chapter up with a moment for self-reflection. You can use the following prompts for journaling or at least take some time to consider the answers.

- When was the last time you felt deeply understood by someone? How did it make you feel?

- What steps have you taken to truly understand someone else's perspective?

- What barriers are preventing you from being more empathetic?

- When was the last time someone showed you empathy and understanding? How did this affect your relationship?

- List three things from your week that could be cultivated into interesting stories.

- Reflect on a time when you didn't agree with someone. How did you handle the situation?

One final question to ask yourself as we reach this point is what other challenges you are facing with communication. Now that you have the foundations for effective communication, it's a good opportunity to explore obstacles that may hinder the amazing progress you are making!

Unlock the Power of Generosity

Giving is not just about making a donation. It is about making a difference.

—Kathy Calvin

People who give without expecting anything in return live happier lives and often achieve more. So, let's try to make that happen during our time together.

To do that, I have another question for you...

<u>Would you help someone you've never met, even if you never got credit for it?</u>

Who is this person, you ask? They are like you. Or, at least, like you used to be. Less experienced, wanting to make a difference, and needing help, but unsure where to look.

My mission is to make talking to anyone easy for everyone. Everything I do stems from that mission. And the only way for me to accomplish that mission is by reaching... well... everyone.

This is where you come in. Most people do, in fact, judge a book by its cover (and its reviews). So here's my ask on behalf of a struggling communicator you've never met:

Please help that person by leaving this book a review.

Your gift costs no money and takes less than 60 seconds to make real, but it can change a fellow communicator's life forever.

Your review could help...

...one more person find the confidence to speak up.

...one more shy individual make a new friend.

...one more professional ace that important presentation.

...one more family member connect more deeply.

...one more dream come true.

To get that 'feel good' feeling and help this person for real, all you have to do is... and it takes less than 60 seconds... leave a review.

Simply scan or click the QR code below to leave your review:

If you feel good about helping a faceless communicator, you are my kind of person. Welcome to the club. You're one of us.

I'm even more excited to help you talk to anyone, anytime, anywhere, more easily than you imagine. You'll love the tips and strategies I share in the coming chapters. Thank you from the bottom of my heart. Now, let's get back to it.

Your biggest fan, Chris

PS - Fun fact: If you provide something of value to another person, it makes you more valuable to them. If you'd like goodwill straight from another communicator - and believe this book will help them - send it their way.

Chapter 6
Overcoming Common Communication Challenges

The biggest communication problem is we do not listen to understand. We listen to reply.
—Stephen R. Covey

In a recent survey, 30 percent of businesses felt that communication had become more challenging in the last year alone (Project.co, 2024). These challenges that impede effective communication come at a cost and not just for companies. Think about the amount of wasted time you have experienced because of the challenges you faced, the misunderstandings, and the stress that comes with all this. The good news is that in the past, communication itself was a challenge. Now, we can work on specific issues that may give your confidence a knock.

Handling Awkward Silences with Grace

Silence often carries a sense of awkwardness that can unsettle the most seasoned conversationalists. It's something we often fear because it implies we have run out of things to say. During silence, emotions and thoughts have a habit of running wild, fueling the fear that we are doing it all wrong, or worse, we are about to be rejected!

However, what if we could reframe the way we view these quiet moments? Instead of seeing them as awkward pauses, we can view them as natural parts of any meaningful dialogue, giving space for the words just spoken to resonate and for new thoughts to form. In practice, this means when you encounter silence, you can use it as a moment to reflect on what has been discussed, gather your thoughts, or even observe the non-verbal cues that can give more insight into the conversation. This approach not only eases any internal pressure to 'fill the void' but also enriches your engagement with the dialogue.

The burning question is how to know when a pause for silence is beneficial and when it actually becomes awkward. In general, a moment of silence should be no more than a second. Think of it as enough time to take a breath. However, this breath should never be a sigh. When silence lasts for more than four seconds, there is a strong chance that one or both of you will start to feel the awkwardness.

Here are some tactics to break a silence that goes on for too long:

- Reintroduce a previous topic that was particularly engaging or bring up a related subject. This can be especially helpful if the silence follows a complete topic wrap-up. You might transition by saying, "Going back to what you mentioned earlier..." Give a compliment followed by a question, for example, "I love your earrings. Where did you get them?
- Use reflective questions or comments. For instance, if a pause

follows a shared personal story or opinion, reflecting back on what you heard can show active listening and encourage further elaboration. You might say, "It sounds like that was a really pivotal moment for you. Could you share more about how it influenced your decisions afterward?"

- Ask questions that generate a story. This goes back to the open-ended questions that allow for a more expansive response and, therefore, more opportunities for follow-up questions.

- Answer questions in depth so that the other person has more to work with. Then, finish with a question so they know where to pick up the conversation. In more personal or sensitive conversations, allowing silence after a significant point lets the gravity of the words sink in, giving the other person space to process their thoughts and feelings.

Don't always be too quick to end a silence because it can be a powerful communication tool. In negotiations or discussions where power dynamics are at play, maintaining composure during silent moments can convey confidence and assertiveness. It shows you are comfortable with silence, which can unnerve others who are less secure.

Before practicing your own pauses in conversation, observe how others use them. Be sure to pay attention in a wide range of settings as well as different people. Notice how long it takes for you to feel any awkwardness and look out for signs like touching the face, avoiding eye contact, and fidgeting as cues that the other person is feeling the same.

The ARE Method for Keeping Conversations Flowing

Imagine you're in a conversation that starts to stall, the topics seemingly exhausted, and you're both hovering on the edge of an awkward silence. This is where the Anchor, Reveal, Encourage (ARE) method comes into play, a simple yet effective framework to keep the conversational ball rolling and even push it into more meaningful territory (McKay & McKay, 2021).

As you read through the ARE steps, take some time to make notes of how this strategy could work for you.

Step 1: Anchor the conversation by connecting with something relevant from the discussion or relating to a topic of known interest to the other person. This could be a comment they made earlier or a topic you know they are passionate about. For example, if someone mentioned enjoying hiking, you might anchor the conversation by bringing up a recent popular trail discovery or asking about their most memorable hiking experience.

Step 2: Reveal something about yourself related to the anchor. This could be your own experience or thoughts related to the topic at hand. By revealing, you are not just sharing information but are also opening the door to your world, inviting deeper connections. For instance, following the hiking topic, you might share your experience on a challenging trail and what it taught you about resilience or the beauty of unplanned detours.

Step 3: Encourage the other person to share their thoughts, feelings, or stories related to the reveal. This could be through questions that invite them to expand on their experiences or simply expressions of genuine interest in hearing more about their views. Encouragement should be open and inviting, making the other person feel valued and interested in diving deeper. For example, you might say, "That sounds like an intense hike! How did you feel when you reached the summit?" Encouragement fosters a sense of companionship and curiosity, key ingredients for a flowing and dynamic conversation.

One of the most significant impacts of the ARE method is its ability to facilitate deeper, more meaningful conversations. By moving seamlessly from anchoring to revealing and encouraging, you create a natural progression that invites both breadth and depth. It transforms conversations from superficial exchanges to profound discussions, where personal insights, emotions, and stories enrich the dialogue, making it more rewarding for everyone involved.

Dealing with Difficult Conversations and Conflicts

Sometimes, just thinking about having to address uncomfortable topics or disagreements can cause stress levels to spike. As tempted as you are to avoid conflict, it's only going to make the situation worse by leaving things undealt with.

Preparing mentally and emotionally before diving into these talks is crucial. Start by setting clear intentions. Ask yourself what you hope to achieve. Is it to clear up a misunderstanding, find a solution to a problem, or simply express your feelings about something that's bothering you? Clarifying your goals can help steer the conversation and prevent it from veering off into less constructive territory.

Visualization is another powerful strategy. Picture the conversation unfolding positively, with both parties listening respectfully and working toward a resolution. This mental rehearsal can boost your confidence and reduce anxiety. As we previously saw with visualization, it can also help you explore potential problems that may come up within a conflict and the chance for you to plan out different ways to handle these issues.

Also, consider jotting down key points you want to cover. This doesn't mean scripting the conversation—which can make interactions feel stiff and unnatural—but having a clear outline in mind can help you stay focused and calm, especially when emotions start to run high.

When you're actually in the midst of these conversations, navigating them with compassion and clarity can make all the difference. It starts with active listening. Sometimes, simply feeling heard can de-escalate a potential conflict and open the door to mutual understanding. Employing empathetic language also helps. Phrases like "I understand where you're coming from" or "It makes sense you'd feel that way" can validate the other person's feelings and lower defenses, paving the way for a more constructive dialogue.

Expressing disagreement constructively is all about the how, not just the what. Critique ideas, not people. For instance, instead of saying, "You drive me crazy when you do that," you might say, "I feel angry when you do that." This approach allows you to take responsibility for your emotions while keeping the conversation focused on resolving issues rather than attacking personal characters. Be mindful of your tone and body language as well. An open posture and calm, steady voice convey respect and willingness to find common ground, even when you disagree.

How would you handle these conflicts?

1. Your colleague isn't pulling their weight in a project and even taking credit for your work.

2. Your neighbor works nights and comes home at 5 a.m., where they start to bang around the place and wake you up...every day.

3. Your partner believes in giving your children' time outs,' but you don't.

4. A customer calls you in a rage because they have been sent the wrong item.

5. Your friend accuses you of flirting with their partner even though you see no change in your behavior.

6. Your sibling borrowed money from you, and instead of paying you back, they are wasting money on stupid things.

Once you have considered how you would verbally respond in these situations, you can take it to the next level and ask someone else to role-play these situations with you so you can work on tone of voice and body language. It's the feedback that you give each other that will really enable you to tweak and master conflict-resolution skills.

Responding to Criticism Without Becoming Defensive

Criticism, whether it lands in your inbox as a professional email or is voiced over coffee with a friend, often triggers an instant and deep-seated defensive reflex. It's natural; no one relishes the idea of being told they've fallen short. However, not all criticism is bad. Constructive criticism, often rooted in a genuine desire to foster growth, comes with an intent to improve your skills or outcomes. It's typically specific, actionable, and delivered with a tone of respect. On the other hand, destructive criticism may feel more like an attack, lacking in specifics and potentially infused with dislike or even contempt, offering little in terms of pathways for improvement.

You might be tempted to dismiss destructive criticism, but before you do, consider who is providing the feedback. Is it someone who knows what they are talking about, or is it someone who takes pleasure in destroying the confidence of others? If the criticism is coming from a respected person, put those empathy skills to good use. It might be that they are trying to deal with their own problems, and they weren't able to express their feedback in a constructive way. In this case, you can ask for feedback to turn their destructive criticism into constructive and usable advice. Distance yourself from those who only give you toxic feedback, and if this happens in the workplace, you should document each case and take it to HR.

Understanding the critic's intent can profoundly transform how you receive their feedback. When criticism is constructive, it's a golden opportunity for personal or professional development—it's like having a coach on the sidelines giving you pointers to refine your game. By shifting your perspective to view criticism this way, you not only reduce the sting but also open yourself up to opportunities that might propel you forward. For instance, if a supervisor points out an error in your project report, recognizing their intent to improve your work can change your reaction from one of embarrassment or irritation to gratitude for the chance to learn and correct your course.

Managing your emotional response to criticism is where mindfulness comes into play. The moment criticism hits, taking a deep, deliberate breath can center your thoughts and prevent an instinctive snap-back. This pause, often no more than a few seconds, allows you to process the initial wave of emotion—be it surprise, disappointment, or indignation—and respond thoughtfully rather than react impulsively.

Once you've steadied your emotional bearings, the next step is to engage constructively with the criticism. Start by acknowledging the feedback received without agreement or defense. A simple "I appreciate your feedback" sets a collaborative tone. Clarifying questions can be incredibly useful here—they help you understand the specifics of the criticism and demonstrate your openness to dialogue. Ask for examples or further explanation to ensure you fully grasp the concerns raised. For instance, if criticized about a perceived lack of engagement during team meetings, you might ask, "Could you give me an example of when you felt I wasn't engaged enough?" This not only shows your willingness to understand but also helps you gather the precise information needed to improve.

By integrating these approaches, responding to criticism becomes less about guarding your ego and more about embracing growth. It transforms potentially uncomfortable encounters into valuable learning experiences, enriching your personal and professional journey with every piece of feedback you courageously confront.

Adjusting Your Communication Style Across Cultures

Diversity, equity, and inclusion are hot topics in the workplace at the moment, and for good reason. Businesses that place emphasis on diversity make better decisions 87 percent of the time, are 35 percent more productive, and have 2.5 times higher cash flow per employee (LinkedIn Learning Hub). For society, diversity reduces biases and stereotypes while increasing empathy and connections. To reap the benefits of diversity in all settings, it's crucial to adjust your communication style so that everyone feels genuinely included.

Cultural sensitivity starts with the understanding that what's considered polite or normal in one culture can be completely different in another. We previously saw how maintaining strong eye contact might be viewed as a sign of confidence and honesty in many Western cultures; in some Asian cultures, it can be seen as confrontational or disrespectful. It's about recognizing that every culture has its own set of values, communication styles, and behaviors that are deeply rooted in its history and societal norms. By approaching these differences with respect and openness, you not only avoid misunderstandings but also enrich your own experience by learning from a spectrum of perspectives.

To effectively adapt to various cultural norms, start by doing your homework. Before engaging in significant interactions with people from a different culture, take the time to learn about their cultural norms and communication styles. This could involve researching online, talking to people who are part of that culture, or even engaging in cultural sensitivity training if available. Pay attention to aspects like verbal and non-verbal communication preferences, attitudes toward hierarchy and authority, and norms surrounding personal space and physical contact.

Here are some simple ways that you can adapt your communication style while respecting cultural norms:

- **Don't make cultural assumptions.** While there are general culture norms you can research, it would be wrong to assume that individuals have the same beliefs, manners, or communication styles based on those you have met from the same culture.

- **Ask people how they like to be addressed.** In some cultures where hierarchy is emphasized, some people may prefer to be addressed by surnames rather than first names.

- **Speak clearly and not rushed.** Even if someone is fluent in your language, it may still be their second language, and they might find it more difficult to understand you if they are feeling stressed or nervous.

- **Match your emotional energy.** Cultures such as Latin America and the Mediterranean tend to be more energetic with their energy and gestures. Matching their energy can help foster a connection.

- **Avoid slang, idioms, and complex language structures.** A lot of these types of language don't translate well and can leave a person feeling confused and isolated.

- **Be careful with humor.** What's funny in your culture may not be in another; it may also be inappropriate or offensive.

- **Stick to one subject at a time.** Make sure one subject is completely wrapped up before moving onto the next. This will involve active listening to ensure the other person has any doubts resolved.

- **Ask single questions.** Allow the other person to answer one question and then ask a second rather than combining questions together.

- **Encourage and respect.** Speaking in a foreign language can make people feel shy and even socially anxious. Use your communication to put them at ease and respect the effort they make.

Finally, it's important not to take some of these tips to the extreme. When traveling through Europe, a friend of mine encountered a little old lady who insisted on speaking incredibly slowly and even shouting. He politely had to remind her that he was American, not deaf or stupid. You don't want to simplify things to the extent you are talking down to people. To gauge this, have a look online for videos of English and non-English speakers in conversations.

Cultural Sensitivity Quiz

You may think that you are quite culturally sensitive, but through no fault of your own, you have overestimated your abilities. After all, it's not something we often take time to reflect on. On a scale of 1 to 5, with 1 being strongly disagree and 5 being strongly agree, consider the following statements:

1. I have positive feelings toward people from other cultures.

2. I am aware of my open cultural behaviors in terms of communication.

3. I regularly provide positive responses to those I interact with from different cultures.

4. I am open-minded with regard to different cultures.

5. I respect the behavior of people from different cultures.

6. I respect different cultural values.

7. I am able to see when I have upset or offended someone from another culture.

8. I can confidently speak to others from different cultures.

9. I feel sociable with people from different cultures.

10. I am able to pick up on subtle differences in our communication.

Did you know that there are more than 3,800 different cultures in the world (IsAccurate, 2021)? It's unrealistic to expect yourself to master the differences of each single one. It's also unrealistic to expect to never make a mistake. Two techniques that we have already mastered will help in these potentially awkward situations. Show your vulnerable side by admitting when you make a mistake, and don't forget the power of a genuine apology.

Looking ahead, the next chapter will delve into strengthening digital communication skills, an essential aspect of our increasingly connected world. Here, we'll explore how to effectively convey your message across digital platforms, ensuring clarity and impact in every interaction, whether it's via email, social media, or virtual meetings.

Chapter 7
Cultivating Digital Communication Skills

The great myth of our times is that technology is communication.

—Libby Larsen

It's important to clear up one thing before we begin. Technology has certainly helped us to be able to communicate with more people around the world, but technology isn't the same as communication. Communication still requires a unique set of skills for it to be effective. In our modern era, digital communication is not just a tool; it's a lifeline to personal and professional worlds. Whether you're tweeting, emailing, or posting, the way you communicate digitally can open doors to opportunities or close them just as quickly.

Digital Communication Fundamentals

From the morning scroll through emails to the evening catch-up on social media, each swipe, click, and tap is a form of interaction. This digital dialogue has become as crucial as face-to-face interactions, sometimes even more so, especially in professional settings where a significant portion of networking, negotiations, and collaborations happens online. The ability to convey your thoughts and feelings accurately without the aid of vocal tones or facial expressions is a skill of immense power.

However, this form of communication isn't just about exchanging information; it's about making connections. Each email, post, or message adds to the larger picture of your personal or professional image. How you articulate ideas, respond to inquiries, and engage with comments shapes how others perceive you in the digital world.

For the 18-35 age group, often dubbed digital natives, the stakes are particularly high. This demographic not only grew up with digital technology but also entered professional fields where digital proficiency is expected. From securing a job through LinkedIn to engaging with global colleagues via Slack, the ability to navigate these platforms proficiently is integral. Moreover, as this demographic often leads the charge in setting new trends and standards in digital communication, mastering this skill set is not just beneficial but essential.

So, how do you take the traditional communication skills, clarity, empathy, and conciseness and adapt them to a digital format? It begins with understanding the strengths and limitations of digital platforms. For instance, email is great for detailed messages but might not convey urgency as effectively as a phone call. Social media allows for broad reach but can dilute personal connections if not handled carefully. Recognizing the appropriate tone and format for different digital mediums is key.

Adapting these skills also means being mindful of the digital footprint you leave. Every tweet and every status update contributes to an online persona that can have a lasting impact. It's about being clear and concise, yes, but also about being thoughtful and intentional with your words. The digital world is swift; words, once posted, are difficult to retract. Learning to pause before hitting 'send' or 'post' can be the difference between a successful exchange and a regrettable one.

Crafting Compelling Digital Correspondence

Have you ever sent a message that was taken the wrong way? Maybe your joke didn't land as intended, or what you thought was a straightforward email was perceived as harsh.

This is where the mastery of tone becomes crucial. The tone in digital correspondence is like the undercurrent of a river; it's not seen, but it guides the direction in which your conversation flows. Crafting the right tone starts with an understanding of your audience and the context of your interaction. A message to a close friend might be casual and littered with emojis, but that tone would likely be inappropriate in a professional email to a senior colleague.

To navigate this, imagine you're speaking with someone face-to-face. Would you use a certain phrase in a real conversation with this person? This mental exercise can help you gauge the appropriateness of your tone. Additionally, reading your message aloud can be a revealing test. If it sounds harsh or overly casual when spoken, it might be worth revising. Remember, digital communication often lacks the immediate feedback of face-to-face interactions, so erring on the side of clarity and professionalism is typically your safest bet.

Speaking of clarity and conciseness, they are your best allies in the digital world. In an era where everyone is bombarded with information, getting your message across quickly and clearly not only shows respect for your recipient's time but also increases the likelihood that your message will be understood and acted upon as intended. Start with the most important information and keep your sentences short and to the point. Avoid jargon unless you are certain the recipient understands it. Keeping messages short can improve clarity, and personal touches can add significant value to your digital correspondence. They transform your messages from generic text into a personal conversation. For instance, mentioning a previous interaction or a shared interest can remind the recipient of your existing relationship and set a positive, collaborative tone. This can be particularly effective in professional settings, where building and maintaining relationships is key. For example, starting an email with "I hope you enjoyed the conference last week; I found your insights on project management particularly enlightening..." immediately personalizes the message and frames the conversation positively.

As email is one of the most popular forms of communication in the professional world, let's take a closer look at what should be included in an excellent, effective one with this checklist:

- Check the email address of the recipient/s is correct.

- Choose a subject that is short, clear, personalized, not in capital letters, and without too many special characters to avoid the email ending up in a spam folder.

- Begin a formal email with Dear + title + surname. Begin an informal email with Hello + first name.

- State the purpose of your email. For example, "I am reaching out to connect regarding..."

- Provide a brief background that supports the purpose of the introduction, and if you are introducing two parties, explain why you think they should connect.

- Ends with a clear next step, such as suggesting a meeting date or a follow-up call.

- When requesting information, clarity is key. Clearly state what you need and why you need it. Provide a deadline, if applicable, and express appreciation for the help.

- Check that your contact details are correct.

- Check whether any attachments are actually attached and

whether they are the correct attachments.

- Double-check spelling and grammar.

Until this format of writing emails becomes second nature, keep this checklist nearby to ensure steps don't get missed. Because we are often pressed for time when sending emails, we often rush to hit the send button only to have to send follow-up emails for more clarity!

The Etiquette of Online Conversations

Navigating the digital landscape requires more than just knowing how to type a message or send an email; it's about understanding the unspoken rules that govern digital interactions, often referred to as 'netiquette.' Every time you engage online, you're stepping into a virtual room filled with potential professional contacts, friends, and even future employers. How you present yourself in these interactions can open doors or close them tight.

To thrive in this space, understanding the dos and don'ts of digital manners is crucial. For instance, always remember that behind every screen is a person. Keeping your interactions respectful, just as you would face-to-face, lays a foundation for positive digital engagements. This means avoiding typing in all caps, which can come across as aggressive, and steering clear of sarcasm unless you're sure it won't be misinterpreted. Without a vocal tone to give clues, your joke might be taken as an insult!

Responding in a timely manner is another pillar of good digital etiquette. In the fast-paced online world, time is often of the essence. Delayed responses can be interpreted as disinterest or neglect, potentially harming professional relationships or personal connections.

The majority of people expect a reply within 24 hours. Research suggests that 46 percent of customers expect a reply within 4 hours, while 12 percent expect a reply within just 15 minutes (Macdonald, 2023). If a comprehensive response will take time, it's courteous to send a brief note acknowledging the message and stating when you'll be able to respond fully. Consider a quick reply stating, "I received your request and will get back to you with the full details by tomorrow afternoon." This will keep your colleague informed and show your attentiveness to their needs.

In the realm of digital communication, the line between public and private platforms can often blur. Understanding when and how to shift conversations from public platforms like X or LinkedIn to more private channels such as email or direct messages is a key aspect of maintaining professionalism and privacy. For instance, if a discussion on a public forum delves into specifics that might be sensitive or confidential, suggesting a move to a private channel is essential. You might comment, "Let's shift this discussion to email to cover the details more thoroughly," ensuring that sensitive information remains confidential and that the conversation remains productive without airing private details in a public venue.

Now, let's talk about using digital expressions like emojis and GIFs. These can be fantastic for adding a touch of personality and warmth to your messages; however, they should be used judiciously. In professional settings, it's important to gauge the corporate culture and the preferences of your colleagues or clients. While some industries might embrace a casual approach, others might view such expressions as unprofessional. When used appropriately, emojis can soften a request, express solidarity, or even share a light-hearted moment. If you are communicating with people from different cultures, consider whether your choice of emoji or GIF is culturally sensitive.

Similarly, be wary of over-sharing or discussing controversial topics that could alienate your audience, regardless of cultural background. Maintaining a professional tone and keeping your content relevant and respectful helps build a positive digital persona.

Reflecting on your digital communications over the past week can be a revealing exercise. Identify any interactions that could have been improved. Perhaps a reply that was too abrupt or an email lacked a clear call to action. Plan how you could handle similar situations more effectively in the future based on the etiquette discussed here. This regular reflection not only helps you hone your digital communication skills but also ensures that your online interactions are as polished and professional as your in-person ones, solidifying your reputation as a thoughtful and skilled communicator in the digital age.

Navigating the Pitfalls of Digital Misunderstandings

Just like face-to-face communication, you are bound to meet some pitfalls along the way. In fact, without the help of non-verbal cues, these pitfalls may be even more apparent. Let's look at strategies to help mitigate potential digital misunderstandings and problems.

Pitfall #1: Not Clarifying Messages

The key to resolving misunderstandings swiftly is to clarify with precision and patience. Suppose you send an email outlining project details, and the recipient misinterprets your suggested deadlines. Instead of letting frustration take the wheel, respond with a message that seeks to clarify your intentions without sounding defensive. You might say, "Thank you for your quick feedback! To ensure we're on the same page, I intended for the deadlines to be provisional and open for discussion based on team capacity. What are your thoughts on feasible timelines?" This approach clears up the confusion and also keeps the dialogue open and collaborative.

Using specific questions in your clarifications helps narrow down exactly where the misunderstanding occurred and guides the conversation toward resolution. This is actually one area of communication where short-answer questions can be beneficial.

Additionally, restating your points in a different way can help. Sometimes, all it takes is a slight rephrasing to make the light bulb flick on. This might involve breaking down complex information into bullet points or providing a summary at the end of a lengthy email, ensuring your key points are understood as intended.

Pitfall #2: Relying on a Cure Rather Than Prevention

To sidestep potential pitfalls, start by previewing your message before sending it. Look for phrases that could be ambiguous or misleading and refine them. Being explicit about your intentions, feelings, and requests can preempt misinterpretations. For instance, if you're sharing feedback in an email, be clear about what you appreciated and what you think could be improved, framing your suggestions positively and constructively.

Adopting a proactive approach by setting expectations at the beginning of your communications can also prevent misunderstandings. For example, if you're kicking off a project via email, outline the communication protocol you intend to follow and invite others to share their preferences. This sets a clear standard for how information will be exchanged and reduces the chances of miscommunication.

Pitfall #3: Ignoring Misinterpretations

When misinterpretations happen, you can't afford to hide behind a screen because they may only escalate into bigger problems! Address them head-on with a blend of empathy and assertiveness. Acknowledge any role you might have played in the confusion and express your commitment to mutual understanding. If the misunderstanding has escalated into a more significant issue, consider shifting to a more personal mode of communication, such as a phone call or a video chat. This allows for real-time interaction and the use of vocal tones and facial expressions to help convey your sincerity in resolving the issue.

Pitfall #4: Forgetting to Follow-up

The art of follow-up is crucial in ensuring that your communications are clear and that any adjustments made are understood and agreed upon. After a misunderstanding has been addressed, sending a concise follow-up message can help confirm that all parties are on the same page. This might be a simple email summary of what was discussed and agreed upon in a resolution call, including any next steps. This not only serves as a written record of the resolution but also reinforces the corrected understanding, ensuring that the same issues don't resurface.

Pitfall #5: Not Protecting Your Online Reputation

In the digital world, vigilance is key. Your online reputation can be your strongest asset or your biggest liability. Regularly monitoring how your personal brand is perceived online can help you manage your reputation effectively. Set up Google alerts for your name and brand, keep an eye on the comments and shares, and engage with your audience consistently. Address negative feedback constructively and professionally, demonstrating your commitment to customer satisfaction and continuous improvement.

Moreover, periodically review your social media profiles to ensure they remain accurate, professional, and reflective of your current career goals and personal values. Updating your bio, profile picture, and portfolio on platforms like LinkedIn can keep your profile fresh and relevant, ensuring that anyone searching for you finds an accurate and positive representation of your brand.

Navigating the digital world requires a keen sense of awareness and adaptability. By mastering these clarification techniques, preventative strategies, and resolution methods, you become more adept at steering clear of the pitfalls that could hinder your communication path. Whether it's through a carefully worded email, a clarifying phone conversation, or a strategic follow-up, each step you take is geared toward building stronger, clearer, and more effective digital interactions.

Virtual Networking: Making Genuine Connections Online

In today's interconnected world, virtual networking has emerged as a pivotal element of professional growth and opportunity creation. Unlike traditional networking, which often requires a handshake or exchanging business cards, virtual networking thrives on digital platforms where your first impression is often made through a profile visit or a well-crafted introductory message.

Effective virtual networking hinges on proactive engagement and strategic interactions. The first step is often making your presence known. This doesn't mean bombarding every new contact with messages, but rather, engaging thoughtfully with content posted by peers or industry leaders you wish to connect with. Commenting with insightful observations or sharing their content with your network can capture their attention and begin a dialogue.

Another strategy involves joining and actively participating in online forums and groups relevant to your field. These platforms are often goldmines for virtual networking, offering a space to share knowledge, ask questions, and connect with like-minded professionals. The key here is consistency; regular engagement helps keep your digital presence active and visible to your network.

When it comes to choosing platforms for professional networking, LinkedIn and X (formerly Twitter) stand out, albeit serving slightly different purposes. LinkedIn is designed explicitly for professional networking and career development. It offers a structured environment where you can showcase your professional accomplishments, join industry-specific groups, and publish articles that reflect your expertise.

On the other hand, X, with its dynamic and fast-paced nature, is excellent for sharing quick updates, joining conversations on trending topics, and directly engaging with leaders and influencers through public replies or direct messages. While LinkedIn remains the go-to for more formal professional interactions, X allows for more casual and immediate connections, often giving you a platform to express your professional opinions and engage in industry discussions in real-time.

The challenge with virtual networking is moving beyond superficial connections to establishing meaningful professional relationships. This transition begins with personalized interactions. When reaching out to a new contact, avoid generic messages. Take the time to review their profile, note any common interests or experiences, and mention these in your communication. For example, if you're reaching out to someone who attended the same university or worked in a similar industry, mention this shared background as a conversation starter. This personalized approach shows genuine interest and increases the likelihood of a positive response.

After the initial contact, maintaining the connection requires regular interaction. Comment on their posts, congratulate them on professional milestones, and share relevant information that might interest them. Over time, these repeated positive interactions can transform a loose connection into a meaningful professional relationship, one that's mutually beneficial.

Navigating virtual networking also demands a good grasp of online etiquette. This includes understanding the appropriate tone and frequency for your messages, respecting privacy, and being mindful of different time zones. Professionalism is key, even in more casual interactions on platforms like X. This means using proper grammar, avoiding overly casual language, and keeping your messages concise and to the point. Additionally, being responsive is crucial. If someone reaches out to you or replies to your message, aim to respond promptly. This shows respect for the other person's time and demonstrates your reliability as a professional contact.

Virtual Networking Event Exercise

To put these strategies into practice, consider setting up a mock virtual networking event. You can use platforms like Zoom or Microsoft Teams to create a simulated networking environment. Invite peers to participate, assigning each participant a role or industry position. During the event, practice introducing yourself, engaging in small talk, and exchanging information as you would in a real virtual networking event. Focus on initiating conversations, asking insightful questions, and following up on discussions. After the exercise, gather feedback from participants on your communication style, the effectiveness of your networking strategies, and areas for improvement. This hands-on practice can significantly boost your confidence and refine your virtual networking skills while also supporting your colleagues' learning.

Virtual Conversations: Best Practices for Digital Communication

Each platform, be it a video call software or a team chat tool, comes with its own set of rules and best practices. For instance, the direct and sometimes informal communication style that works in team chat apps like Slack may not be appropriate for more formal video conferencing tools like Zoom or Microsoft Teams used during client meetings or executive presentations.

To excel in video calls, it's crucial to maintain a professional demeanor, just as you would in an in-person meeting. This means being punctual, dressing appropriately, and ensuring your environment is free from distractions. On video calls, your visual presence speaks volumes before you even say a word. Moreover, maintaining eye contact with the camera (not the screen), nodding to show you are listening, and using hand gestures moderately can significantly enhance your presence and engagement.

Conversely, when using team chat tools, the dynamics shift. Here, clarity and brevity lead the way. Quick, clear responses are valued, and the use of specific channels or threads keeps discussions organized and accessible. Emojis and GIFs, when used sparingly, can help in adding tone to your messages, making your intent clearer and the conversation lighter. The key lies in adapting your communication style to fit the platform while maintaining professionalism and respect for the conversation and your counterparts.

Another effective technique for formal and informal occasions is the strategic use of multimedia tools to create more engaging and personable interactions. This could involve sharing your screen to walk through a presentation visually, using digital whiteboards for collaborative sessions, or even sending personalized video messages instead of standard emails for more impact. These tools can help simulate the face-to-face experience, making digital interactions more dynamic and engaging.

Emerging Technologies in Digital Communication

As digital landscapes evolve, so do the tools we use to communicate within them. Technologies like virtual reality (VR) and artificial intelligence (AI) are setting new frontiers for digital communication. VR meetings, for example, are no longer sci-fi fantasies. They are real tools that can transport meeting participants into a 3D environment where they can interact with each other as if they were in the same physical space. This technology can revolutionize how we conduct remote meetings, offering a level of interaction and engagement that closely replicates in-person dynamics.

AI-driven analytics is another game-changer, especially in understanding and enhancing audience engagement. AI tools can analyze communication patterns, suggest optimal times for posting on social media, or provide insights into the types of content that generate more engagement. Implementing these tools can help tailor your communication strategies effectively, ensuring your messages are not just sent but also well-received and impactful. Furthermore, they can save you a lot of time!

These technologies, while advanced, are becoming increasingly accessible, making now the perfect time to start exploring and integrating them into your communication strategy. Whether it's adopting VR for remote team meetings or using AI to analyze customer interactions on social media, staying ahead of these trends can provide you with a significant advantage in both personal and professional realms.

Mastering digital communication is about much more than staying connected—it's about making every interaction count. By adapting to different digital platforms, leveraging psychological techniques, and embracing emerging technologies, you can overcome the barriers of distance and create meaningful, impactful connections. Looking ahead, the next chapter will explore how these digital skills not only enhance personal interactions but also amplify your professional capabilities in a digital-first world.

Chapter 8
Building and Maintaining Personal and Professional Relationships

We have two ears and one mouth so that we can listen twice as much as we speak.

—Epictetus

It's the moment of first contact that can be both daunting and brimming with possibility. Here, in these initial seconds, lies the opportunity to build a connection that could open doors to new friendships, career opportunities, or enriching conversations for years to come. This chapter is all about mastering the art of making quick, genuine connections—whether you're at a fast-paced networking event, a casual meet-up, or anywhere in between.

Building Rapport Quickly: Strategies for Immediate Connection

You may think that every time you meet someone, you have a few minutes to make that all-important first impression. You have approximately 7 seconds before the other person has formed an opinion of you and vice versa. That's barely enough for a smile, handshake, and saying your name. Further research has shown that the brain can map snap judgments about people in just a split second (Jaramillo, 2020), a process known as thin-slicing.

Thin-slices are like snapshots that integrate and process information, allowing a person to come to a basic conclusion about another person's character. These snapshots include facial expressions, body language, and tone of voice. Thin-slicing can be surprisingly accurate. One study had participants watch 5-second video clips and 5-minute video clips and make observations on macro traits such as likeability, trust, competence, nervousness, and sympathy, as well as micro traits like smiling, eye contact, open-handed gestures, and fidgeting. There was no difference in observations for macro traits after watching the 5-second clip and the 5-minute clip, although the micro traits were harder for people to identify (Thompson, 2012). This implies that our thin-slicing can be helpful when forming general opinions of others.

On the other hand, the process of thin-slicing can hinder our ability to form accurate first impressions. Part of the brain that is involved in first impressions, the prefrontal cortex, is also involved in biases (Mcleod, 2024). It's possible that in these few seconds, your brain is making a first impression; it's also tapping into past information and experiences and using them to influence your current decisions. Because the brain also makes an emotional connection to a first impression, it can be very hard to change! While all of this is happening, the other person's brain is doing exactly the same.

For a relationship to be maintained and even flourish, you need to make the most of your 7 seconds!

- **Adjust your attitude**. Before approaching someone, make a conscious decision to leave your stress and negative thoughts behind and adopt a friendly attitude that will be shown through your body language.

- **Change your posture**. Raise your shoulders toward your neck, then back, and allow them to drop down. This is a good posture to show openness.

- **Smile before you approach a person**. Rather than just smile when you meet someone, make sure you are smiling before you approach because the brain is more likely to respond positively. You can always increase your smile when you come face-to-face, as long as it's not fake.

- **Ask yourself: What color are their eyes?** The ideal amount of eye contact when you first meet someone is enough to notice the color of their eyes.

- **Flash your eyebrows.** Not in a seductive or suspicious way, but a brief eyebrow raise can show signs of friendliness.

- **Use your space wisely.** Though you should maintain the right amount of space so as not to make the other person feel uncomfortable, slightly leaning in shows you are engaged in what they have to say.

You will notice that, unlike many other books and sites, I haven't included a handshake in the ideal first impression. Personally, I would follow the lead of the other person when it comes to shaking hands. Aside from cultural differences, since the pandemic, the use of handshakes has very much changed!

With so little time, active listening can seem like a challenge. However, a condensed version of active listening can be incredibly effective. This involves quickly picking up on key phrases or emotionally charged words that the other person uses and reflecting them back to show understanding and engagement. For example, if someone mentions they're 'overwhelmed' by a new project, you might respond with, "It sounds like you've got a lot on your plate with this new project. What's the biggest challenge you've faced so far?" This shows that you're listening and also that you care enough to delve deeper into their experience.

In the next sections, we'll explore how to maintain and nurture these connections over time, ensuring that the seeds you plant in these first crucial moments can grow into lasting personal and professional relationships.

Maintaining Long-Term Relationships Through Effective Communication

Navigating the waters of professional relationships requires more than just making a good first impression; it demands a strategic and ongoing effort to keep those connections alive and beneficial. When you think about your career as a garden, networking is not just about planting seeds; it's about nurturing those plants to bear fruit in the future. This means every interaction, every follow-up, and every introduction is a deliberate step toward advancing your career goals.

Strategic networking involves identifying not only who can help you but also how you can add value to their professional life, creating a mutual benefit. This requires a deep understanding of your own career goals and the industry landscape. Before stepping into any networking event, have a clear idea of what you're aiming to achieve. Are you looking for a mentor, seeking insight into another industry, or trying to land a new client? With this clarity, you can navigate toward individuals and conversations that align with these objectives, making the most of each interaction.

Introductions are your gateway to new relationships. In professional settings, where first impressions are crucial, crafting an introduction that is memorable and impactful is key. Start by clearly stating who you are and what you do, but go beyond the basics. Share a snippet of your professional journey or a recent accomplishment that sparks interest. If you are uncomfortable sharing accomplishments or worried you will come across as bigheaded, mention something your team has achieved, changing "I" to "we." There comes a moment in many professional interactions when exchanging contact information is the next natural step. However, the way you request this information can significantly impact the other person's willingness to stay in touch. Always ensure that the request is timely—ideally when both parties have expressed a clear interest in continuing the conversation or when a potential opportunity to collaborate has been identified. Use polite and considerate language and frame your request in a way that highlights mutual benefits. For example, you might say, "I'd love to share that article we talked about. Could I perhaps get your email to send it over?" A simple phrase like this highlights the valid reason for your request and reinforces your intent to provide value.

The real magic in networking often happens after the initial contact. Following up is where many falter, yet it's crucial for turning brief interactions into lasting connections. Ideally, make sure you follow up with new contacts within 24 to 48 hours. Effective follow-up starts with a timely, personalized message that reminds the recipient of who you are and what you discussed. It expresses gratitude for your interactions and has a specific request. For example, after meeting someone interested in your project management skills, you might send an email that says, "It was great discussing our shared passion for innovative project management techniques at the conference. I would love to continue our conversation over coffee next week to discuss potential collaborations." This kind of follow-up keeps the conversation alive and shows genuine interest in developing the relationship.

By weaving these strategies into your professional interactions, you not only keep your network vibrant and active, but also ensure that your connections are meaningful and aligned with your long-term career aspirations and growth.

The Role of Empathy in Strengthening Connections

Navigating the subtle yet profound differences between empathy and sympathy can transform your interactions and deepen your connections in both personal and professional realms. Sympathy involves feeling compassion, sorrow, or pity for the hardships that another person encounters. It's a supportive experience where you recognize their distress and provide comfort, but you do not necessarily feel what they're feeling. Empathy, on the other hand, goes a step further. It's about stepping into the shoes of another person, truly understanding their feelings and perspective as if they were your own. This doesn't mean you need to have experienced exactly what they have, but rather that you connect with the emotions they're experiencing.

Why is empathy so crucial for meaningful connections? Because it signals to others that their feelings and experiences are seen and valued. It creates a safe space for vulnerability and honest sharing, which is the foundation of any strong relationship. When you empathize, you're effectively saying, "I see you, I hear you, and what you feel matters to me." This can significantly enhance trust and openness in your interactions, making it easier to navigate even the most challenging conversations. Empathy allows for a deeper understanding and appreciation of diverse viewpoints and experiences, fostering a culture of respect and inclusiveness.

Often, in conversations, especially in professional settings or when we're in problem-solving mode, there's a tendency to jump straight to solutions. This approach, while well-intentioned, can sometimes overlook the importance of simply understanding the other person's perspective or emotional state. It's crucial to distinguish between offering solutions and providing understanding. When someone shares a problem, before jumping to solve it, ask yourself if they might need empathy and validation more than immediate solutions. If you are unsure, ask if they would like your advice before assuming.

Providing understanding involves active listening, acknowledging the emotions involved, and validating the person's experience without immediately trying to fix the issue. This approach can be profoundly impactful because it gives the individual space to feel understood and supported, which is often what they need to find clarity and solutions themselves. It also prevents the potential frustration that can come from feeling unheard or having one's feelings overlooked. For instance, if a colleague is stressed about a looming deadline, instead of suggesting time management tools right away, a more empathetic approach could be to first acknowledge their stress and explore what's contributing to it.

Difficult conversations, whether they're about conflicting views, feedback, or sensitive topics, can significantly benefit from empathy. It can be a powerful tool in de-escalating tension and finding common ground. When disagreements arise, try to understand the emotions and motivations behind the other person's viewpoint. This doesn't mean you have to agree, but understanding can reduce the emotional charge and lead to more constructive solutions. For example, in a heated debate about a project direction, expressing empathy for a colleague's concerns can open up a pathway to compromise: "I understand you're worried this approach might be too risky. Let's explore how we can mitigate potential problems."

Setting and Respecting Boundaries in Relationships

Think of boundaries as invisible lines that help define how much you are willing to give and receive in relationships, ensuring that interactions remain respectful and mutually beneficial. Understanding and communicating these boundaries effectively can prevent misunderstandings and conflicts, making your relationships healthier and more sustainable.

- **Physical Boundaries**: personal space and physical touch

- **Intellectual Boundaries**: respect for ideas, opinions, and beliefs

- **Emotional Boundaries**: sharing the right amount of information, having your emotions validated

- **Sexual Boundaries:** the right to say no, expressing sexual likes and dislikes, and respecting limitations

- **Material Boundaries:** related to your money and possessions, what you are willing to share or lend

- **Time Boundaries**: Make sure you use your time in a healthy way, saying no when necessary so that you have time for each aspect of your life.

Recognizing your own boundaries is the first crucial step in setting them. This involves deep self-reflection to understand what you are comfortable with, how much you are willing to tolerate, and where you draw the line in different aspects of your life. For instance, you might be okay with a coworker calling you during weekends for urgent matters but not comfortable with regular weekend work calls. In a friendship, you might find it draining to provide constant emotional support, but be happy to offer advice when specifically asked. Identifying these limits is not about building walls but rather about knowing yourself well enough to communicate your needs and expectations clearly. This clarity helps in managing your energy and commitments, ensuring you engage in relationships that respect your values and limitations.

Consider the answers to these self-reflection questions to get a better understanding of your boundaries.

- What things do you struggle to say no to?

- List your most important values.

- When do you find it hard to talk about your needs?

- Describe a moment when you felt disrespected.

- What parts of your life need more attention?

- What feels heavy in your life right now?

- Imagine your ideal boundaries in different types of relationships; what do they look like?

- What are your personal non-negotiable limits?

Once you're clear about your boundaries, the next step is to communicate them effectively. The key here is to be assertive yet respectful, ensuring that your tone and choice of words convey your needs clearly without offending the other person. For example, if a colleague has a habit of dropping by your desk often to chat, and it affects your productivity, you might say, "I really enjoy our chats, but I find I work best with fewer interruptions. Could we perhaps catch up during lunch breaks?" This approach acknowledges the value of the interaction while also setting a clear boundary. When communicating boundaries, be direct and use "I" statements to express how certain behaviors affect you and suggest reasonable alternatives that work for both parties.

Just as you set your own boundaries, respecting others' boundaries is equally important. This involves paying attention to verbal and non-verbal cues that indicate others' comfort levels and adjusting your actions accordingly. If someone seems uncomfortable with a particular topic, it's wise to steer the conversation elsewhere. If a friend mentions they need some space, honor that request without taking it personally. Respecting others' boundaries shows that you value their feelings and comfort, which can strengthen the trust and longevity of your relationships.

Despite your best efforts, there will be times when your boundaries are tested or violated. When this happens, addressing the issue promptly and clearly is critical. Let the person know which boundary has been crossed and how it made you feel. Reiterate your boundary and the importance of respecting it. If the violations continue, consider if further action needs to be taken, such as spending less time with the person or, in more serious cases, ending the relationship. It's important to protect your well-being, and sometimes that means making tough decisions about who you allow into your personal or professional space.

Setting and respecting boundaries not only safeguards your personal well-being but also enhances the quality of your relationships. By clearly understanding and articulating your own limits, you invite others to interact with you in a respectful and mindful manner, creating a healthy foundation for any relationship. As you navigate through various interactions, remember that boundaries are not barriers but rather expressions of self-respect and mutual respect that are vital for any healthy relationship.

As we reach the final chapter, I want you to take a moment to appreciate and celebrate how far you have come. Over the last eight chapters, you have gone from extreme shyness and even social anxiety to being able to assertively communicate and enforce boundaries in your life. Though these strategies will require ongoing practice, your biggest hurdles have been overcome. The only thing left is to explore a few more advanced communication techniques for diverse scenarios and even more meaningful connections.

Chapter 9
Specialized Communication Strategies for Unique Situations

Communication works for those who work at it.
—John Powell

As promised, you were going to master the art of talking to anyone, and this chapter ensures you have what it takes to have an open conversation with the teenager who only grunts at you in a conference room full of your esteemed colleagues. Let's begin by building on those crucial first 7 seconds!

The Elevator Pitch: Communicate Your Value Quickly

Imagine your elevator pitch as a mini advertisement of yourself, one that's concise yet packed with compelling details that capture your essence. The key elements of a powerful elevator pitch include clarity, brevity, a hook, and a specific task or goal.

- Clarity is paramount; your pitch should quickly and clearly communicate who you are, what you do, and what unique value you bring.

- Brevity is your friend here. Aim for about 30 seconds, enough to spark interest but not overwhelm.

- Your hook, or the opening line, should grab attention and make the listener want to learn more.

Finally, end with a specific task or goal, whether it's setting up a meeting, gaining a referral, or simply exchanging contact information.

The effectiveness of your elevator pitch can dramatically increase when you tailor it to your specific audience. Consider who you're speaking to and what their interests or needs might be. For a potential employer, focus on your skills and achievements relative to the industry. For an investor, highlight what makes your business idea unique and profitable. Switching up a few details to align with your audience's interests can make your pitch more relevant and engaging. In personal interactions, focus on finding your common ground.

Practice your elevator pitch in a multitude of settings: networking events, conferences, social gatherings, or even during unexpected encounters like a coffee shop run-in with a potential client. In each scenario, be mindful of context and adapt your delivery accordingly. At a networking event, you might go into more detail, while a chance meeting might call for a more casual approach. Always be prepared to expand on your pitch if the situation allows, providing more details about your experience and aspirations. With practice and adaptability, you'll be able to use this tool effectively across various settings, ensuring you always leave a memorable impression.

Public Speaking Tips for the Socially Anxious

Transforming anxiety into a powerful presentation is not just possible; it's profoundly rewarding. This section delves into effective strategies to prepare mentally and physically, captivate your audience, manage in-the-moment nervousness, and continuously improve your public speaking skills.

The foundation of a great speech is laid long before you step onto the stage. Preparation is twofold: Mental and physical. Mentally, start by understanding the core message of your speech and the key takeaways for your audience. This clarity will not only boost your confidence but also ensure your message is coherent and impactful. Visualization is a powerful tool here. Spend time imagining a successful presentation, seeing yourself speaking confidently and your audience reacting positively. Physically, prepare your body to perform at its best. Practice deep breathing exercises to calm your nerves and ensure your voice is steady. Engage in moderate exercise on the day of the speech to boost endorphins, enhancing your mood and energy levels. Also, pay attention to your diet; avoid heavy meals that might make you sluggish and opt for light, energy-boosting foods instead. Make sure to hydrate well— a dry mouth is a common response to nervousness and can be distracting during a speech.

Once on stage, your primary goal is to connect with your audience. This connection is the key to keeping them engaged. Start with a strong opening—a surprising statistic, a provocative question, or a compelling story to grab attention and set the tone for the rest of your presentation. Use clear and expressive language and vary your tone to maintain interest. Make eye contact with different parts of the audience as you speak, making sure all your listeners feel included.

Incorporating interactive elements can also enhance engagement. This could be as simple as asking rhetorical questions, encouraging audience participation through the show of hands, or using tools like real-time polls if you're using digital presentation software. These strategies can break the monotony of a one-way speech and keep your audience actively involved in your presentation.

It's natural to feel nervous, but how you manage these feelings can define your speaking experience. First, accept that nervousness is a normal part of public speaking; this acceptance alone can reduce its power over you. Remember how we used the name it to tame it technique and how the power pose can reduce the stress hormone cortisol? Also, focus on your breathing; slow, deep breaths can help maintain a calm demeanor and steady voice.

Another effective strategy is to focus outwardly rather than inwardly. Shift your attention from your anxieties to your message and the audience's learning. Remember, your presentation is not about proving yourself but about conveying valuable information or insights to your listeners. This perspective shift can significantly reduce pressure and redirect your energy toward delivering a meaningful speech.

To practice public speaking beforehand, consider joining a local or online public speaking group like Toastmasters, which offers a supportive environment to practice and receive feedback. These groups not only provide a platform for regular practice but also help you observe and learn from others.

By embracing these strategies, you can navigate the challenges of public speaking with greater ease and effectiveness. Remember, every speaker has room for improvement, and every speech is an opportunity to grow. With preparation, engagement, and a focus on continuous improvement, you'll not only enhance your public speaking skills but also turn what was once a source of anxiety into a powerful tool for personal and professional growth.

Communicating in High-Stakes Situations

When the stakes are high, the room feels different. Your heart might race a bit faster when you're about to propose a new business idea to potential investors or when you're leading a crisis management team during an unexpected company emergency. These scenarios are what we call high-stakes situations. Here, your words carry weight, and your communication style can make or break the outcomes you're striving for. The key in these moments is not just to communicate but to do so with precision, confidence, and adaptability.

High-stakes situations require a meticulous approach to preparation. This isn't just about rehearsing your points but about knowing your material inside and out. This deep familiarity frees you from the confines of memorization and allows you to deliver your message with confidence and clarity. Begin by structuring your content clearly—have a strong opening that outlines your main points, support these points with solid data or anecdotes, and conclude with a compelling call to action. Use tools such as cue cards or slides with key bullet points to keep you anchored during your delivery, ensuring you cover all critical aspects without being tied to a script, which can feel unnatural.

Rehearsing in an environment that simulates the real setting can be incredibly beneficial. For instance, if you're preparing for a critical board meeting, practice in a conference room with colleagues who can role-play as board members. Encourage them to interrupt with challenging questions or express skepticism so you can practice maintaining composure and steering the conversation back to your agenda.

Moreover, enhancing your verbal and non-verbal communication skills can significantly impact your delivery. Speak clearly and at a measured pace to ensure your message is understood. Make deliberate eye contact to connect with your audience and use purposeful gestures to emphasize key points.

Listening actively and adjusting your message based on the feedback you receive during these interactions is crucial. Pay close attention to the reactions and responses of your audience. Are they confused, intrigued, or perhaps skeptical? This feedback is invaluable as it allows you to tailor your message and address concerns directly, enhancing the effectiveness of your communication. For instance, if you notice confusion, you might pause to clarify a point before moving on. If there's skepticism, provide additional evidence to support your claims or address potential doubts proactively.

Following up after high-stakes interactions can solidify your message and reinforce your professional relationships. Send a thank-you email summarizing the key points discussed and the next steps, or provide additional resources that support your message. By integrating these strategies into your preparation and execution, you equip yourself to handle high-stakes communication scenarios with greater skill and confidence, which will help you deliver your message effectively and achieve the outcomes you desire.

Communicating Effectively in Romantic Relationships

The core principles of healthy romantic communication, honesty, openness, and empathy, are pivotal. Honesty fosters trust and respect, which are cornerstones of any lasting relationship. When you're honest, you create an environment where your partner feels safe to be open and honest in return. Openness involves being forthcoming with your feelings and thoughts. It's about sharing your inner world, your dreams, fears, and desires, which can be incredibly vulnerable but also deeply bonding. Empathy, the ability to understand and share the feelings of another, allows you to connect with your partner's experiences on an emotional level, bridging gaps of misunderstanding and creating a supportive and nurturing environment.

One of the most challenging aspects of any relationship is navigating conflict effectively. Conflict, when handled constructively, can strengthen your bond rather than weaken it. The key is to focus on the issue at hand and avoid personal attacks. Begin by expressing your feelings using "I" statements rather than "you" statements, which can sound accusatory and escalate the conflict. For instance, saying, "I feel hurt when plans are canceled at the last minute," centers your feelings and invites resolution, rather than "You always cancel our plans," which might provoke defensiveness. Always strive to listen first to understand rather than to respond. This shows respect for your partner's perspective and opens a dialogue that focuses on resolution. Remember, the goal is not to win an argument but to solve a problem together.

Expressing needs and desires clearly and respectfully is another pillar of healthy romantic communication. It's important to know and communicate your boundaries and expectations in a relationship. Clear communication about what you need and desire, be it emotional support, personal space, or physical affection, helps prevent feelings of neglect or frustration. Approach these conversations with a clear, calm mind and a firm understanding of what you need to feel fulfilled and happy in the relationship. It's equally important to be receptive to hearing and understanding your partner's needs and desires. Finally, choose the timing of these conversations wisely. They should be had when both of you are in the right, relaxed mind frame rather than, for example, when you both get home from a long day, and you are exhausted.

By embedding these principles into your everyday interactions, you set a powerful precedent for your relationship's communication dynamics. This doesn't just apply to the big moments or the deep conversations; it's equally important in the daily exchanges, the small gestures, and the casual chats.

Strategies for Communicating with Children and Teenagers

Communicating effectively with children and teenagers is not just about talking to them—it's about connecting with them on their level, understanding their world, and guiding them as they grow. In many ways, empathizing with children is harder than it is with adults because it's harder to put ourselves in their shoes. Most of us would give anything to go back to the school days when responsibilities were few and less demanding. But this isn't a fair approach because children, especially teens, are living in a world that is very different from when we were children. It's important to respect their struggles and challenges and validate their feelings!

The journey starts with tailoring your communication to match the developmental stage of the child or teenager. For younger children, this means using simpler language and concrete concepts. Your body language and tone should be open and inviting, encouraging them to express themselves. It often helps to physically get down to their level so you aren't dominating space. With teenagers who have a greater capacity for abstract thinking, you can employ more complex language and discuss more abstract concepts like justice, freedom, or love. This doesn't mean you should talk down to younger kids or be overly formal with teens; rather, it's about finding the right balance that respects their intellectual level and emotional maturity. For instance, when explaining why they need to do homework, you might tell a younger child that it's like the practice needed to be good at a game, whereas for a teenager, you could discuss how it prepares them for college and future career opportunities.

Adjusting your tone, body language, and facial expressions also plays a crucial role in effective communication with kids and teens. Younger children respond well to warm, enthusiastic tones and expressive gestures, which help hold their attention and convey affection. Teenagers, although they might seem to prefer less overt displays of emotion, still need to feel understood and respected. This means maintaining eye contact, nodding to show you're listening, and keeping your tone respectful. These non-verbal cues can help strengthen your connection, making your verbal communication more effective.

Creating an environment where children and teenagers feel safe and comfortable sharing their thoughts and feelings is crucial. Regularly scheduled "talk times" can be incredibly effective. These are specific times set aside each day or week dedicated solely to talking about whatever is on their minds. During these sessions, it's important to put aside distractions like phones or other tasks and give the child or teenager your full attention. This signals that their thoughts and feelings are important and that there is always a safe space for them to express themselves. Over time, these sessions can greatly increase their comfort in sharing and strengthen your relationship.

Active listening during these conversations shows that you value what they're saying. Reflect back on what you hear without immediately jumping in with advice or judgments. For example, if your teenager is talking about a conflict with a friend, resist the urge to solve the problem for them. Instead, respond with something like, "It sounds like you were really upset when Eve decided to hang out with someone else. How are you feeling about it now?" This approach not only validates their feelings but also encourages them to process their emotions and think critically about their own responses, skills that will benefit them throughout their entire lives.

Clear boundaries and expectations are fundamental in any relationship, providing a sense of security and stability. When setting boundaries with children and teenagers, it's important to be clear and consistent but also to explain the reasons behind these rules in a way they can understand and accept. For younger children, boundaries might be simple, like not hitting others or needing to hold your hand when crossing the street, explained in terms of safety and care. For teenagers, you might set boundaries around curfew or internet use, discussing the reasons related to trust and responsibility.

When communicating these boundaries, use a firm but gentle tone, making sure they understand that these rules are for their well-being and that they are part of a loving and caring relationship. It's also important to be willing to listen to their side and negotiate when appropriate. When children feel like they are part of the decision-making process, they are more likely to respect the boundaries.

Teaching children and teenagers to express their emotions in healthy ways is a vital part of their development. Encourage them to name their feelings and express them verbally. This could be as simple as starting with statements like "I feel..." in response to different situations. For younger children, you might use games or storytelling to help them identify and name different emotions. For teenagers, encourage journaling or art as outlets for their feelings.

Building emotional resilience is equally important. This involves helping them to see failures or setbacks as opportunities to learn and grow. Encourage a growth mindset that views challenges as a normal part of life and focuses on the effort rather than the outcome. For example, if your child does poorly on a test, instead of focusing on the grade, discuss what they learned from the experience and how they can improve next time.

If there is one thing I wish I had been taught at school, it would have been emotional intelligence along with resilience. Never in my life have I needed to list the capital cities around the world or recite the digits of pi. However, every single day of my life, I have interacted with humans! I have needed to understand all the emotions involved in a conversation and how I can use that emotional awareness to improve my communication. Sharing these skills with children sets them up for a brighter future, where communication won't ever be the same obstacle as it has been for you.

Conclusion

The quality of your communication is the quality of your life.
—Anthony Robbins

As we wrap up our journey through "The Art of How to Talk to Anyone," I want to take a moment to reiterate the core mission of this book. My aim has always been to empower you to transform your communication skills. This guide has been meticulously crafted to boost your confidence across various social situations, especially if you've ever felt held back by social anxieties or believed you weren't capable of forging deep, meaningful connections.

From the basics of overcoming social anxiety and breaking down the communication process to mastering small talk and enhancing non-verbal cues, we've covered a broad spectrum of tools and strategies. These are your keys to not just surviving but thriving in both personal and professional interactions.

Every technique and strategy has made a significant difference to my communication abilities, but there are a few things that particularly stood out in terms of improving my confidence.

The first was the science behind social anxiety and how it was actually a way for my body to protect me. Relaxation, along with exposure therapy, was the first noticeable step to overcoming what was originally blocking attempts at interactions, let alone effective communication. As soon as I was able to manage my anxiety, I was able to start making far better use of those all-important 7 seconds, which gradually became an impactful 1-minute elevator pitch. Then came the power of those open-ended questions, and I started to feel genuine connections with others.

Active listening wasn't too much of a challenge for me, but I confess mastering non-verbal cues took a little longer. I wasn't always confident in recognizing subtle cues, so I decided to take a step back, not put so much pressure on myself, and focus on easier things to notice, such as the Duchenne smile, posture, and fidgeting. Once I felt these skills improving, I went back to paying more attention to things like micro-expressions. This reinforced a valuable lesson for me— not everything has to be achieved at once!

Methods like SYNC GOALS, TED, ARE, and SHARE were brilliant structures that helped provide my brain with a plan, whether that was for my motivation or for improved focus when needed to pay attention to formulating conversations rather than letting my emotions take over. My own emotional regulation laid the foundations for seeing other's perspectives and considering how they really felt in different situations.

Today, I am confident that I can communicate well, but I also appreciate that with every new person I meet, I may need to tweak my approach! I encourage you to keep practicing, experimenting, and learning. Use the tools and strategies we've discussed in various contexts, from casual chats at the coffee shop to high-stakes business meetings. Don't be discouraged by setbacks; instead, view them as opportunities to refine your skills further.

As we part ways on this page, carry with you not just the knowledge but the confidence that you are well-equipped to navigate the world of interpersonal communication. You have the tools, the techniques, and the inner strength to make meaningful connections with anyone you meet.

I have one final ask of you! So many other people are currently overwhelmed by anxiety and their lack of communication skills, and it's holding them back. By sharing your reviews on Amazon, I get to hear about your success stories, but more importantly, your opinions show others that there is a solution available for them to break free from their fears, communicate with confidence, and achieve their dreams. It takes less than 60 seconds and a few clicks, and I will be extremely grateful.

On that note, here's to your future filled with rich, rewarding conversations and relationships.

Keeping the Game Alive

Thank you for considering leaving a review. Now that you have the tools to talk confidently to anyone, it's time to share your newfound knowledge and show other readers where they can find the same help.

Simply by leaving your honest opinion of this book on Amazon, you'll show other aspiring communicators where they can find the information they're looking for and pass on their passion for effective communication.

Thank you for your help. The art of communication is kept alive when we pass on our knowledge – and you're helping me do just that.

Simply scan or click the QR code below to leave your review:

References

Accelerated Urgent Care. (2024, March 14). *Beyond small talk: Conversation starters to conquer social anxiety.* Accelerated Urgent Care. https://accelerateurgentcare.com/2024/03/14/beyond-small-talk-conversation-starters-to-conquer-social-anxiety/

American Psychological Association. (n.d.). *Shyness.* https://www.apa.org/topics/shyness

Blain, T. (2023, May 11). *The importance of mindful communication for mental health.* Verywell Mind. https://www.verywellmind.com/mindful-communication-definition-principles-benefits-how-to-do-it-7489103

Brett, M., & Mitchell, T. (2022, May 11). *How to build strong business relationships — remotely.* Harvard Business Review. https://hbr.org/2022/05/how-to-build-strong-business-relationships-remotely

Calm Editorial Team. (2024, February 8). *7 deep breathing exercises to help you calm anxiety.* Calm Blog. https://www.calm.com/blog/breathing-exercises-for-anxiety

Carey, E. (n.d.). *7 steps to stand out at networking events.* Hult International Business School. https://www.hult.edu/blog/networking-7-steps/

Carney, D., Cuddy, A., & Yap, A. (2010). *Power posing: Brief nonverbal displays affect neuroendocrine levels and risk tolerance.* Psychological Science, 21(10), 1363–1368. https://doi.org/10.1177/0956797610383437

Castrillon, C. (2021, January 21). *How to craft a knockout elevator pitch.* Forbes. https://www.forbes.com/sites/carolinecastrillon/2021/01/21/how-to-craft-a-knockout-elevator-pitch/

Coppell, R. (2024, April 24). *15 TED questions for customer service – with examples.* Call Centre Helper. https://www.callcentrehelper.com/ted-questions-customer-service-examples-202868.htm

Covey, S. R. (1989). *The 7 habits of highly effective people.* Simon & Schuster.

Cuncic, A. (2020, September 16). *Positive affirmations for social anxiety.* Verywell Mind. https://www.verywellmind.com/how-can-i-talk-to-myself-in-a-positive-way-3024821

Cuncic, A. (2024, February 12). *7 active listening techniques for better communication.* Verywell Mind. https://www.verywellmind.com/what-is-active-listening-3024343

Gould, W. R. (2023, March 7). *Why vulnerability in relationships is so important.* Verywell Mind. https://www.verywellmind.com/why-vulnerability-in-relationships-is-so-important-5193728

Hunkins, A. (2022, September 15). *The #1 obstacle to effective communication.* Forbes. https://www.forbes.com/sites/alainhunkins/2022/09/15/the-1-obstacle-to-effective-communication/

IsAccurate. (2021). *Cultures around the world: customs, norms, and other differences.* https://isaccurate.com/blog/cultures-around-the-world

Jaramillo, J. (2021, October 22). *The science and power of first impressions.* University of Melbourne Science Communication Blog. https://blogs.unimelb.edu.au/science-communication/2021/10/22/the-science-and-power-of-first-impressions/

Jorfi, H., Saeid, J., Hashim, G., & Bin, J. (2014, October). *The impact of emotional intelligence on communication effectiveness: Focus on strategic alignment.* ResearchGate. https://doi.org/10.5897/AJMM2010.036

Joubert, S. (2019, November 12). *How to improve cross-cultural communication in the workplace.* Graduate Blog. https://graduate.northeastern.edu/resources/cross-cultural-communication/

Kalaba, J. (2021, November 23). *Should you use emojis in business communication?* Pumble Blog. https://pumble.com/blog/emojis-business-communication/

Kaspersky. (2023, September 8). *What is netiquette? 20 Internet etiquette rules.* https://usa.kaspersky.com/resource-center/preemptive-safety/what-is-netiquette

Kindig, C. (2018, December 3). *What it takes to create community connection. Foundation for Intentional Community.* https://www.ic.org/create-community-connection/

Kramer, L. (2023, June 14). *How to write a professional email, with tips and examples.* Grammarly. https://www.grammarly.com/blog/professional-email-in-english/

Kuhnke, E. (2011, May 10). *Kinesics: the categories of gesture.* Elizabethkuhnke's Blog. https://elizabethkuhnke.wordpress.com/2011/05/10/kinesics-the-categories-of-gesture/

Lee, E. (2023, April 20). *Effective questioning.* CPD Online College. https://cpdonline.co.uk/knowledge-base/business/effective-questioning/

Leverage Edu. (2023, December 7). *Barriers of communication: What is communication? and effective ways to improve communication.* Leverage Edu. https://leverageedu.com/blog/barriers-of-communication/

Lifesize. (2021, March 24). *Video conferencing best practices.* https://www.lifesize.com/video-conferencing/video-conferencing-best-practices/

LinkedIn Learning. (n.d.). *Why is diversity and inclusion important?* https://learning.linkedin.com/resources/learning-culture/diversity-workplace-statistics-dei-importance

Lucas, R. (n.d.). *Nonverbal communication quote - Peter F. Drucker.* Customer Service Skills. https://www.customerserviceskillsbook.com/wordpress/nonverbal-communication-quote-peter-f-drucker/

Lumen. (n.d.). *Cultural context.* https://courses.lumenlearning.com/suny-esc-communicationforprofessionals/chapter/cultural-context/.

Malhotra, D. (2014, April). *15 rules for negotiating a job offer.* Harvard Business Review. https://hbr.org/2014/04/15-rules-for-negotiating-a-job-offer

Mayo Clinic. (n.d.). *Fear ladder building: Getting started.* https://anxietycoach.mayoclinic.org/anxiety/building-a-fear-ladder/

Marie, S. (2022, April 18). *8 ways to build vulnerability in relationships.* Psych Central. https://psychcentral.com/relationships/trust-and-vulnerability-in-relationships

McKay, B., & McKay, K. (2021, June 6). *Social Briefing #7: How to initiate small talk using the ARE Method.* The Art of Manliness. https://www.artofmanliness.com/people/social-skills/social-briefing-7-initiate-small-talk-using-method/

Mcleod, S. (2024). *Thin-slicing judgments in psychology.* Simply Psychology. https://www.simplypsychology.org/thin-slicing-psychology.html

Mehrabian's 7-38-55 communication model: It's more than words. (n.d.). *The World of Work Project.* https://worldofwork.io/2019/07/mehrabians-7-38-55-communication-model/

Midjourney. (2024, May 22). *AI-generated image.* Midjourney. https://www.midjourney.com

Mindful Staff. (2018, December 12). *How to practice mindfulness.* Mindful. https://www.mindful.org/how-to-practice-mindfulness/

Morillo, E. (2023, December 2). *74 technology quotes to inspire innovation.* Gracious Quotes. https://graciousquotes.com/technology/

Mullenweg, M. (2015, March 15). Technology is best when it brings people together. Interview in *TechCrunch.*

NeuroLeadership Institute. (2020, September 17). *The neuroscience of laughter, and how to inspire more of it at work.* https://neuroleadership.com/your-brain-at-work/neuroscience-laughter-at-work/

Newell-Legner, R. (n.d.). *How to SOFTEN Up Your Fans.* 7 Star Service. https://www.7starservice.com/articles/how-to-soften-up-your-fans

OpenAI. (2024). *Images created using DALL-E* (15 images). https://www.openai.com/dall-e

OpenAI. (2024). *Images created using DALL-E, modified by the author* (2 images). https://www.openai.com/dall-e

Perera, K. (2022, March 3). *Positive visualization exercises and techniques to try now.* More Self Esteem. https://more-selfesteem.com/more-self-esteem/self-confidence-tips-2/self-confidence-and-optimism/visualisation-for-confidence/

PiAcademy. (n.d.). *Importance of voice modulation and tone in public speaking.* PiAcademy Tutors. https://piacademy.co.uk/advice/voice-modulation/

Pogosyan, M. (2017, June 29). *Non-verbal communication across cultures. Psychology Today.* https://www.psychologytoday.com/us/blog/between-cultures/201706/non-verbal-communication-across-cultures

Powell, J. (1969). *Why am I afraid to tell you who I am?.* Argus Communications.

Project.co. (2024). *Communication statistics 2024.* https://www.project.co/communication-statistics/

Raeburn, A. (2023, September 9). *11 places where eye-contact is not recommended (11 places where the locals are friendly)*. TheTravel. https://www.thetravel.com/10-places-where-eye-contact-is-not-recommended-10-places-where-the-locals-are-friendly/

Rakel, R. E. (2012). *Proxemics: spatial factors*. In Elsevier eBooks (pp. 115–126). https://doi.org/10.1016/b978-0-12-411577-4.00010-1

Ramki, H. (2023, November 28). *11 actually great elevator pitch examples and how to make yours*. Zapier. https://zapier.com/blog/elevator-pitch-example/

Raypole, C. (2021, September 17). *How CBT can help you manage social anxiety symptoms*. Healthline. https://www.healthline.com/health/anxiety/social-anxiety-disorder-cognitive-behavioral-therapy

Robbins, A. (1991). *Awaken the giant within*. Free Press.

Roychowdhury, D. (2024, March 8). *The power of visualization: Enhancing performance in sport and exercise*. Dr. Dev Roychowdhury. https://www.drdevroy.com/visualization-in-sport-and-exercise/

Selva, J. (2018, March 16). *Challenging negative automatic thoughts: 5 worksheets (+PDF)*. PositivePsychology.com. https://positivepsychology.com/challenging-automatic-thoughts-positive-thoughts-worksheets/

Smith, M., & Segal, J. (2024, February 5). *Social anxiety disorder*. HelpGuide.org. https://www.helpguide.org/articles/anxiety/social-anxiety-disorder.htm

Smokovski, L. (n.d.). *Bearded man talking to a young female seated on a banner [Photograph]*. Adobe Stock. https://stock.adobe.com/au/images/bearded-man-talking-to-a-young-female-seated-on-a-banner/292237540

Stachowiak, D. (2022, February 19). *11 ways to facilitate great conversations*. Coaching for Leaders. https://coachingforleaders.com/facilitate-great-conversations/

Stillman, J. (2023, October 20). *Learn the FORD method and never struggle to make small talk again*. Inc. https://www.inc.com/jessica-stillman/learn-ford-method-never-struggle-small-talk.html

SuperOffice. (2023, September 1). *7 ways to reduce customer service response times*. https://www.superoffice.com/blog/response-times

Suttie, J. (2017, July 17). *How laughter brings us together.* Greater Good. https://greatergood.berkeley.edu/article/item/how_laughter_brings_us_together

Sutton, J. (2021, July 6). *How to perform assertiveness training: 6 exercises.* PositivePsychology.com. https://positivepsychology.com/assertiveness-training/

Thompson, J. (2012, March 24). *Thin slices & first impressions.* Psychology Today. https://www.psychologytoday.com/intl/blog/beyond-words/201203/thin-slices-first-impressions

Top 12 communication problems quotes. (n.d.). A-Z Quotes. https://www.azquotes.com/quotes/topics/communication-problems.html

Torre, J. B., & Lieberman, M. D. (2018). *Putting feelings into words: Affect labeling as implicit emotion regulation.* Emotion Review, 10(2), 116–124. https://doi.org/10.1177/1754073917742706

University of New Hampshire. (2023, July 24). *Communication: The method matters.* Psychological & Counseling Services. https://www.unh.edu/pacs/communication-method-matters

Van Edwards, V. (2024, April 19). *The definitive guide to reading microexpressions (facial expressions).* Science of People. https://www.scienceofpeople.com/microexpressions/

Vojkovsky, R. (n.d.). *Open-ended questions: 28 examples of how to ask properly.* Customer Happiness Blog. https://www.nicereply.com/blog/open-ended-questions-examples/

Weber, G. (2014, September 5). *Affirmations: Do they work for anxiety and low self-esteem?* HealthyPlace. https://www.healthyplace.com/blogs/treatinganxiety/2014/09/positive-affirmations-do-they-really-work-for-anxious-people-with-low-self-esteem

Westover, J. H. (2023, September 13). *The art of emotional control: Strategies for managing emotions during challenging discussions.* HCI Consulting. https://www.innovativehumancapital.com/post/the-art-of-emotional-control-strategies-for-managing-emotions-during-challenging-discussions

Yuko, E. (2024, January 17). *Use the "FORD" method to master small talk*. Lifehacker. https://lifehacker.com/health/master-small-talk-ford-method

Zak, P. J. (2014, October 28). *Why your brain loves good storytelling*. Harvard Business Review. https://hbr.org/2014/10/why-your-brain-loves-good-storytelling

Zucchet, E. (2023, August 22). *Body language in different cultures around the world: A top guide*. Berlitz. https://www.berlitz.com/blog/body-language-different-cultures-around-world#

Made in the USA
Las Vegas, NV
06 February 2025

17655953R00079